Arthur H. MacOwen

**A Thousand Miles with the Queer Quartette**

Arthur H. MacOwen

**A Thousand Miles with the Queer Quartette**

ISBN/EAN: 9783337324292

Printed in Europe, USA, Canada, Australia, Japan

Cover: Foto ©Thomas Meinert / pixelio.de

More available books at **www.hansebooks.com**

A

# THOUSAND MILES

WITH

# THE "QUEER QUARTETTE."

BEING AN ACCOUNT OF

A TRIP BY BICYCLE AND BOAT FROM THE CITY OF PHILADELPHIA
TO THE WHITE MOUNTAINS AND RETURN,
BY WAY OF

## LAKES GEORGE AND CHAMPLAIN.

BY

## CHRIS WHEELER.

PHILADELPHIA
AMERICAN ATHLETE PUBLISHING COMPANY,
1218 Filbert Street.
1891.

# PREFACE.

Merely as a matter of form, and not by any means as a necessity, is the inevitable Preface placed here in its time-honored position. All that need be said is, that if the facts here related—and nothing but facts are related in this book—give pleasure to the friends for whom they are put into this form, then the object of the "Quartette" in thus boldly sending them abroad in print has been realized.

CHRIS WHEELER.

WEST PHILADELPHIA, Nov. 1st, 1891.

# A THOUSAND MILES

## WITH THE QUEER QUARTETTE.

Before having anything to do with the "Thousand Miles," it may be as well to briefly introduce the "Queer Quartette" to those who feel enough interest in them or their doings to follow their wanderings as described in the following pages.

The "Quartette" was composed of four Philadelphia cyclers, Mr. H. L. Roberts, Mr. Gilbert F. Wiese, and Mr. Arthur H. MacOwen, members of the Pennsylvania Bicycle Club, and Mr. Chester Roberts, a younger brother of the first-named gentleman. That they were a "Queer Quartette" will be sufficiently evidenced before their story is fully told, and a very brief personal mention of each in advance will suffice for the needs of a formal introduction. That a formal introduction is necessary is accounted for by the fact that Mr. Roberts, Sr., is a great stickler for the proprieties—this is not casting any reflection on the general make-up of Mr. Roberts, Jr., or the rest of the party—and he will no doubt feel more at his ease on being introduced as "Laurie," which *Annie*, one of his friends, will recognize as his distinctive pet name. He is tall and spare, and you would never take him to be a cycling traveler, but what his form lacks in volume it more than makes up in muscle. He wears whiskers when he permits and cultivates their growth, and a mustache always; the only things which he carries about with him as constantly and faithfully as the same mustache being his ever-present attribute of kindly good nature and an ever-ready ability to eat. One other feature of his personality must not be overlooked. His camera is as much a portion of himself as are his hands, only perhaps more so, for he never forgets that he owns a camera. Only one more of genial "Laurie's" good points need be noted—he has an eye for the ladies, and two eyes for the very pretty ladies, and when he divests himself of his hirsute chin ornaments it really does seem as though the ladies have a partiality for him.

Perhaps we should have first introduced our youngest companion in arms. Chester Roberts is what a mutual male friend termed a "dandy," and what a gushing young lady defined as a "daisy." Exactly how the two terse summings up apply as describing accurately one individual is a problem to be worked out by our readers, if they have the inclination and possess the patience to follow the "Quartette" in its ramblings. Chester, who was the pet of the party, is a clean-cut, straight-limbed youth—no reflection intended anent the limbs of the rest of the party—with the budding promise of a blonde mustache, and with a fully developed sensibility as to the claims which everything beautiful and nearly everything good has up on his attention. Chester is a little less spare and a little less tall than his elder fraternal traveling companion. He has a slightly scientific bent of mind, has read a book or two in his time, and can dance better than he can play tennis, which latter recreation he affects more than cycling. Possessing very taking ways, it early became evident to the other three-quarters of the "Quartette" that it would be advisable in choosing stopping places to select those at which the usual summer-resort state of things existed, viz., a multiplicity of the fair sex, and as much of a paucity as possible of the opposite one. However, taking him all in all, Chester was a very fair fellow, both in face and action, throughout the "Wanderings."

"Say, Chester."

A half-sleepy and wholly-tired "well," from Chester.

"Good-night, Chester." Gilbert F. Wiese formed the third fourth part of our "Quartette," and if we indulged in the prerogative of a son of Hibernia, we would say, he constituted the biggest fourth of the whole. At any rate, he possessed the biggest voice, and whether rendering the sweet modulations of "Annie Laurie," "Steady Boys, Steady," or "Lassie Queenie," or whether howling to be allowed out of the salt water at Newport, on the first acquaintanceship of his life with it, his lung power could always assert itself over any two others of the "Quartette." "Gilbert," or "Gil," which, remembering that brevity is the soul of wit and many other good things, is the name by which his friends know him, is tall and not spare, with a head and face molded on the lines of some of those old statues of Roman patricians—that is, it is round without being bullet-like—and with eyes which, although not Cæsarean, would have stood their owner a fair show with Marc Antony in the good graces of Cleopatra, for "Gil's" optics laugh as well as his lips.

Gilbert never rode a bicycle until three months ago, and he never laid eyes on the ocean until he saw it at Coney Island on the first day of the "Quartette's" wanderings. But if in such matters his education was neglected, like individuals who lack the possession of any one or more of the senses, his mastery of other things is wonderful. Music hath charms for others than the untamed, of course, and certainly it hath charms for Gilbert. Only for his having to carry, most religiously, a package of cigarettes wherever he went, it is fair to suppose that his mandolin would have formed a portion of his traveling outfit.

"Hope deferred maketh the heart sick," and we have no doubt but that our readers have been impatiently waiting to hear what the fourth party of the "Quartette" is like, therefore we hasten to relieve the impatient strain of expectancy by saying that we are an implicit believer in the truth of the old saying that ' the last is always best," and we think this is description enough of the writer.

# CHAPTER II

## THE START.

"Where are you going, my pretty maid?"
"To Coney Island, sir," she said.
"What will you do there, my pretty maid?"
"Why I'll see what the world calls fun," she said.

It had been the original intention to start from Philadelphia on July 4th, but two of the party being detained at the great meet held at Hagerstown, Md., and the other two having ridden several times across New Jersey, it was decided to start from New York on July 5th, and leave the ride between the two great cities of the eastern seaboard until the return trip, and thus preserve as much as possible the schedule of the ride as at first laid down, one of the party having but two weeks at his disposal.

Brightly gleamed the waters of New York Bay as the huge ferry-boat of the Pennsylvania Railroad forged slowly out of her New Jersey dock, and slanted her pug nose across the broad bosom of the Hudson toward Cortlandt Street on the New York side. In the first row of passengers, crowding as American passengers always will, to the front, so as to make time getting off, was the "Quartette," each with his bicycle, and each in the gray habiliments characteristic now of so many of our cycling clubs. In the front of three caps were three silver keystones resting on three little cross-bar squares of blue and gold ribbon, the former the emblem of the Pennsylvania Bicycle Club, the latter mementos of the Hagerstown Bicycle Meet at which the colors of "Pennsy" had been carried in the fashion instanced. On two of the machines cameras were strapped, on one a tripod and "fixings" were securely lashed, and on every one was also a large bundle, encased in a waterproof cover. These bundles, averaging in weight 15 pounds each, with the cameras, constituted all the baggage considered requisite for a trip of from two to three weeks.

"Where are you bound for?" asked an old gentleman, who evidently voiced the wish on the part of the surrounding crowd to know where the squadron of heavy cavalry was bound for.

"The White Mountains," was the answer from the writer followed by the words, "and beyond," from Gil Weise.

"What, on those things?" said the questioner, elevating his eyebrows, and then he added, "and, how far beyond?"

Gil thought that perhaps he was counting his chickens, or, more properly speaking, his miles before they were realized, so he said:

"That depends, sir."

"I should think it does. But I wish you a pleasant trip there and 'beyond,'" said the old fellow, laying the least little bit of stress on the word "beyond."

The crowd looked us all over as the boat ran into the slip, and, no doubt, many of them set us down as of the genus fools, which was rather rough on Gil Wiese, seeing that he formed, as before remarked, the biggest quarter of the "Quartette."

By boat and bicycle to the White Mountains, and as far "beyond" as possible, was the programme of our trip, and the afternoon of the 5th was to see us on board the palace steamer "Pilgrim," en route for Newport. Two of the party, strange to say, had not been in New York before, and,

7

of course, wanted to see everything from the Battery to the far end of Central Park. Such a programme being out of the question for one day, it was resolved to cross the city to the East River Bridge, then across this connecting link between the two great centres of what should be one metropolis, ride through Brooklyn to its beautiful Prospect Park, and from the Park by way of the splendid boulevard to Coney Island, the Brighton of New York. While conversant with all that makes Atlantic City the Brighton of Philadelphia, and, indeed, of a great portion of America, the "Quartette" were wholly ignorant of what Coney Island, which maintains the same relationship with New York, was like, so the wheels were fronted eastward, and the softest Belgian blocks selected until the long rise to the magnificent aerial spans of the Brooklyn Bridge was reached. Over this monument to the engineering genius of the New World passes the great stream of travel between New York City proper and Brooklyn. Steam cars, all kinds of wheel vehicles, and pedestrians cross it, and from the central span, under which large ships can pass without stepping their topmasts, a splendid view is had of the two cities, the bay, islands, and shipping extending for miles in every direction. A halt was made on the centre of the structure, and the camera unstrapped. Along came a large three-master, a barque, and as she passed underneath our feet, the novel sight was caught and kept for reference by our photographer. Down the Long Island side of the bridge there is a slope that is good for a magnificent coast, but several accidents having happened to cyclers who, deceived by what appears but a slight grade, allowed their machines to get from under control, the police have strict orders to prohibit coasting by wheelmen on the bridge. Being strangers we were sampling the lazy man's ride, when "wan of the force" politely informed us we were "brakin' the law," which offense was immediately condoned by braking the machines.

The belgian blocks of Brooklyn are no better than those of New York or Philadelphia, and we had to cover quite a number of them before Schermerhorn Street was reached, and a few asphalt thoroughfares carried us to the entrance to Prospect Park, the pleasure-ground on which Brooklyn prides itself.

Without the ultra cultivation of Central Park, and without the wild, natural beauty of Fairmount Park, Prospect Park has a charm of its own, and approaches more the style of beautiful Druid Hill Park, in Baltimore, than do either the noted New York or Philadelphia pleasure grounds. A long and most enjoyable coast round the side of the lake sent us out toward the gate on the Coney Island side at a rapid rate, and then per the counsel of a local cycler, we followed the sidewalk all the way to Coney Island, a distance of some seven miles. The roadway is good enough, but rather cut up on account of the amount of driving done on it, and no objection is made to wheelmen using the footway, which, for the entire distance, is little better than the ordinary sidepath on a country road running into a country town.

Riding at a fast gait, we were just beginning to think the miles very long when the hotel buildings on the beach came into view ahead and in a very few minutes we were among them and in the precincts of the much talked about and lauded Coney Island.

The said Coney Island is not a patch upon Atlantic City, except in the matter of running beer saloons and keeping concert gardens and theatres open on Sunday. In the matter of size and general make-up, it cannot compare with the great New Jersey summer resort, and to get anything of the better sort of entertainment in the line of creature comforts, as well as a moderate amount of ease or retirement, you have to cross over to Manhattan Beach or Brighton Beach. As for a board-walk, that is a thing the Coneyites don't have.

" Everything goes," as the saying is, at Coney Island, week day and Sunday. There is an endless variety of the stereotyped amusements which the great public never tires of. Merry-go-rounds, toboggans, razzle-dazzle rides, shooting galleries, monstrosity shows, theatrical and acrobatic exhibitions, music, mixed with beer and other things, the big elevator, and the monster elephant, chance games of all descriptions, bathing in all its branches, and in all rigs, etc., etc., etc.

A few pictures of scenes eminently typical of the most democratic of American holiday resorts were imperative and a few were secured, owing to the courtesy of Superintendent R. Schermerhorn, of the Prospect Park and Coney Island Railroad.

It was within five minutes of sailing time when the " Quartette " pulled up at the wharf of the Fall River line of steamers, after pounding for a considerable distance over the New York belgians and cobble-stones, which, so far as softness and smoothness goes, are not a whit more pleasant to ride over than their brothers which make the streets of Philadelphia alike the terror of cyclers and carriage drivers and the pride of city councilmen.

And now we have to recount a curious fact, but before recounting said curious fact, we will record an extremely gratifying one. Upon deciding to start from New York, we also decided to take the Pennsylvania Railroad to that place, and both on the train and in Jersey City, the conductor and also the brakeman of the train, No. 4, were more than attentive, the former opening up a car in which were some of the Columbia College party returning after the boat race the previous day, and the latter waiting a quarter of an hour with us in the depot to see that we got our wheels and baggage on the elevators in the new mammoth terminus that we were strangers to.

This was the gratifying fact, and now we will mention the curious one. The Fall River line charge fifty cents a wheel for the trip between New York and Newport. This seems curious since the large transportation companies carry wheels free. Each bicycle, with what we had on it, weighed less than the regular amount of baggage allowed passengers, and of course we handled them ourselves and they lay up in a corner side by side, taking up but little space, and giving no trouble to either the cloak room or parcel office. The Hudson River boats, on the contrary, do not make any charge for a man's bicycle, neither do the Lake Champlain steamers, so that when a party of wheelmen like the " Quartette " are on a trip it is questionable if it is policy to take the Fall River line if transport is required in the direction we followed.

2

# CHAPTER III.

## ON TO NEWPORT.

All aboard the " Pilgrim "
Steaming fast and free,
Over fair Long Island's
Royal inland sea ;
Jolly boat and cycle
Pilgrims, four are we.

Cloud-tops far to Westward
Lose their amber light,
Hill-tops off to Eastward
Slowly fade from sight,
Jolly boat and cycle
Pilgrims say " Good night."

Long Island Sound is a splendid sail by day, as it is a beautiful one by night when the moon lends its aid to enhance the charms of this *beau idcal* route between the metropolis and the large centres of New England. I have traveled it by day and by night, and when the queen of the dark hours dedicated to repose asserts her right to rule over the calm waters that stretch for 150 miles along the New York and Connecticut shores, the journey over the shimmering wavelets, is an experience which the most prosaic individual cannot make without experiencing some pleasure, be it great or small.

The " Quartette," however, were not favored with the attention of " her most gracious majesty." Slowly the green slopes of Long Island grew more distant, slowly the village-fringed shore of Connecticut receded toward the west, and slowly the shadows dropped over a scene of water, sky, and woodland that is indeed very fair to look upon, while fast sped the great steamboat, the much-talked-about and truly palatial " Pilgrim," toward the haven we desired to reach, the noted Newport.

An adjournment to supper at half-past seven, developed the fact that, trip appetites were coming to the front, and introduced us to the storage capacity, fearful and wonderful in its make-up and extent, of " our Laurie."

Cigarette, stogie, and cigar helped to while away the hours on the upper deck after supper, and the strains of the really good orchestra, which is a feature of travel on this and all the boats of the Fall River line, found their way out of the windows of the main saloon, and set Gil Wiese singing, or trying to sing, for, oppressed with the knowledge that he was on part and parcel of the ocean, our vocal light seemed more inclined to be meditative than musical. By degrees, what looked like low-lying stars peeped out along the water-line ; they were the lights on the far-away shore of Long Island, and ever and anon a cluster would appear on the opposite side showing where some town or village lay on the seaward edge of Connecticut.

Owing to our late arrival we had failed to secure a state-room aboard, every one being taken, and about 10 o'clock, as the great waste of water continually passing away behind us commenced to grow tiresome in the darkness, almost simultaneously the question suggested itself to us all, Well, what are we going to do about it ?

" Let's sit in the saloon all night," suggested Laurie.

" Or on deck," put in Chester.

10

" Yes we will, I'm going to get a bed somewhere if I pay double for it," chimed in Wiese. " I'll go ask the Captain," he added, jumping up as he spoke.

We all commenced to laugh.

" The Captain will refer you to the cook, Gil," said Laurie ; " suppose you try the steward."

Gilbert went off, and had not been gone long when he returned jubilant and smiling, saying :

" Hallo, boys ! let's all sing ' Rock me to sleep, Mother,' I've got the quarters, come see them."

It is needless to say we were not slow in responding.

" There's your couch, fit for an Ottoman Turk," said he, pointing to the upper floor of the grand saloon.

We looked in astonishment along the corridor formed between the ornamental woodwork covering in the engine space, etc., and the long row of state-room doors. On the floor were dozens of improvised beds, made up of a mattress, blanket, and pillow each, and most of them were already occupied, some with wakeful, others with most undoubted—from the noise they made—sleeping travelers. The whole scene looked more like what you would see in a hospital than what you would expect to see on a palace steamboat.

' Any objection to sleep with your feet to the boiler, Chester ?" said Gil, throwing off his coat.

" None in the least, but it's not in there."

" Well, the inwards of the boat are, whether they are the boiler or not, I know there are no berths there, for I looked," said Gil. " This is a free treat, boys, from the Captain, you don't pay anything for this kind of a sleep," he added, as we all commenced to turn in.

This was the case. We paid nothing for our berth, and as we had to get off at two o'clock in the morning, at which time the steamer reached Newport, our missing getting a state-room was not such a severe affliction after all.

" Newport, gents," shouted the colored steward, and with some grumblings at the unearthly hour, we rubbed our eyes, sat up in our not uncomfortable sleeping places, and took a look at the long lines of sleepers upon the floor. Then there was a hustle into our outside garments, which we had discarded for what was a short period of repose, and then a descent to the lower deck for our wheels.

The big boat got slowly up alongside the wharf and in a few minutes we were once more on *terra firma*, feeling very much as if we were strangers in a strange land, at two o'clock in the morning, and also feeling slightly chilly, owing to the sudden transition from our warm quarters aboard the boat to the cool air of a Rhode Island night. Obtaining our bearings from a wharfman, we followed about a quarter of a mile of thoroughfare to the Perry House.

Our time being limited breakfast was ordered early, and then, by the advice of the natives, we took in what is known as the " Ocean Drive," a magnificent stretch of macadamized road running for 10 miles around the town and the coast adjoining. Passing the noted Casino and the Ocean View Hotel en route, we soon found ourselves among the villa residences of the fortunate and wealthy, which make Newport so well known in the realm ruled by money and fashion. The great Vanderbilt marble mansion, now in course of completion, loomed up on our left, and then after a mile or so, we ran out on the coast, and for several miles traversed a succession of small ups and downs, with an extended view of the sea to the left, and to the right, rocky hillocks, farm lands, and handsome summer residences. On returning to the town, Gilbert, who had never tasted the sweets of salt-water bathing, proposed that before dinner we should hunt up the beach and " go in." To reach the bathing place a mile had to be traversed a-wheel, and a local cycler who sported one of Sterling Elliott's hickory bicycles very kindly showed us the way, and then piloted us back. The rider of the hickory product of Newton, Mass., was very curious about the hickory " Common Sense " wheel that wherever our party went drew attention. While we enjoyed the salt water, he tried the Phila-delphia wooden wheel, and said he did not think the "Quaker City " could be as slow as it was generally made out to be. Colder than the water at Atlantic City or the other New Jersey coast resorts, it was a try-ing ordeal to Gil on his first introduction to the embrace of Father Neptune. Although a capital swimmer, try how we would we could not induce the product of the Allegheny and Monongahela Rivers to go be-yond waist deep in the briny pool at Newport.

" Is this what you call salt water, why it is as cold as ice water, ice water that you can't drink, too, that makes it worse ; I'm going out to wait for a better day," shouted he of river water education, and out he went, too. At a later date, however, when you got him in you could hardly get him out of the " ice water."

The cottages at Newport are the great feature of the place, and they bear favorable comparison with the most pretentious of our rich men's suburban residences near Philadelphia, New York, or the other large cities.

It was after three o'clock when we bade adieu to this noted watering place, with its beautiful harbor, its handsome residences, and its historic associations, in connection with the chequered early life of New England, and turning our faces northward took the road up the Island for Fall River, some 18 miles distant on the Massachusetts side. The sun shone with a little more good-will than was exactly comfortable, but from many points on the road we had glorious views of the beautiful land-locked stretch of blue water that forms the highway for vessels from the ocean to Fall River and Providence. The roadway itself was not bad, and no dismounts were in order until within a few miles of Fall River, where, after descending a long and rough surfaced hill, we tumbled into the unwelcome embrace of six-inch deep sand, which extended for a mile along the level of the water which some little time before we had almost lost ourselves in admiring. There is nothing in this world either in the way of pleasure or pain that is not counterbalanced in some way or other by its opposite, although you may not always realize the fact. We fully realized that, in the wealth of sand which we had to sample, there was more than the balance to the pleasure we had derived from the splendid view over the sail-dotted and hill-girdled expanse of beautiful blue water.

A causeway takes you across the narrow portion of the river or inlet, from the Rhode Island to the Massachusetts side, and then you are only a mile from the great manufacturing town of Fall River, and strike very fair roads until you run in on the belgian block pavement of the city proper. We entered the place just about the time that many of the mills were letting out their swarms of employees, and dusty as we were, and burdened with more than the ordinary amount of baggage carried by cycling strollers, the attention of the rank and file of cotton spinners, etc., was of necessity aroused.

The writer carried a valise strapped on the handle-bar of his machine, and the way that machine steered in consequence was, to descend to the vulgar, "a caution." In addition to the weight of mundane cares in the way of baggage, two of the party carried extra weight in the shape of the divine endowment of whiskers, and such attributes of cycling being evidently new to the unsentimental citizens of Fall River, most pointed and not very flattering remarks were passed, not *sotto voce*, either, by those severely practical sons of toil, and presumably true-blue Democrats.

"Look at the man with whiskers riding a bicycle," shouted a young urchin, with a tin dinner-pail swinging in one hand while with the other he pointed with half glee, half ridicule at our dear old Laurie, riding over the hillocks of a not very good road. Everybody within hearing distance who was not looking looked at our little party on hearing this sally. Wiese burst out laughing, and shouted to our vanguard :

"Laurie, you're a marked man ; hold up your head."

The writer laughed also, and then laughed again, but the second time on the wrong side of his mouth, as the same shrill treble, prefacing his exclamation with an expletive, yelled :

"Oh ! here's another on 'em with whiskers ; look at the portmantys, fellers ; get onto 'em. G', ain't they good uns."

He was only a 12-year-old, and must have been English, by the way he spoke. While on the subject, I may add that the facial adornments of two of us seemed a fruitful source of pleasure to the dwellers in a number of places we,struck in this region of what we supposed to be one of the enlightened divisions of this great United States. Whether they do not hold such things at their proper value or not, I cannot say, but, while the feelings of the writer were not exactly hurt, he could not help experiencing some disappointment at finding out that the education of the masses which Massachusetts brags so much about, is not all that it is cracked up to be.

Riding into the centre of the town, which, by the way, is a large and prosperous one, with many fine mills and extensive manufacturing interests, we commenced to look around for our hotel, and while eagerly scanning the names of streets, and looking for signs that would tell us whether the place was "prohibition" or not, a cycler hailed us and inquired if we wanted the L. A. W. stopping-place. On our answering yes, if it was a good house, he directed us to the Mellin House, and we had no reason to regret his kindly courtesy, for we found the place eminently to our taste, and though the most pretentious hostelry in the town, it did not prove too much for our pocket-books. I make this remark because we had started out with half an idea of roughing it—that is, trying if we could not strike places *en route* after the order of the wayside inns of England, where, as a couple of us had experienced, man and beast are well entertained at generally preposterously low prices. Early on our trip, however, we gave up the idea of following this programme on this side the water, and when a town was struck Gil Wiese's first question always was, "Where is the Delmonico's of this city?" while good, patriotic old Laurie would chin in with, "No, Gil, no; not 'Del's.' What is 'Del's.' Where's the place that's the nearest thing to Boldt's that can be gotten in this centre of Eastern civilization ?"

Well, we had fun, even if sometimes it was at the expense of the whiskered battalion, and at the expense of Eastern education.

After supper we strolled out to see what was going on without the hotel, and were scarcely 50 yards from our temporary home when we were accosted by one of the natives, who turned out to be a cycler like ourselves, and a member of the Fall River Bicycle Club.

" Are you the gentlemen who are touring from Philadelphia ?" he asked, in a way that stamped him at once, not as an inquisitive Yankee, as we had been brought up to believe all Yankees are, but after a fashion that at once impressed us that he was a friend and a brother.

An affirmative answer being given to his query, the next step was an introduction by him to several other gentlemen with whom he had been talking prior to our advent on the scene, and then an adjournment to the cozy quarters of the Fall River Bicycle Club, close at hand, where we found that body of active wheelmen in session, at their regular business meeting. They would by no means hear of our retiring, so we at once became part and parcel of the gathering, and heard the various little things touching the eligibility of this party and that prior to election to membership, which our own experience of club life in Philadelphia made so familiar to us. The meeting did not last long, and then we found what a nest of good fellows we had tumbled in amongst. We carry many pleasant memories of that evening's chat about old-time cycling experiences, and all the rest of those things wheelmen delight in raking up from the past, and won't forget in a hurry D. T. Johnson or Frank Nicolls or Frank Burgess, or the rest of them, and may we get to Fall River again some-time, even if some of the public school graduates did " get on to " per-sonal charms which they did not themselves possess. On parting from our friends—too early they said, but we had work before us next morning—nothing would do but that they should send a party to speed us on our way, and, sure enough, promptly on time, Mr. Johnson, Mr. Nicoll, and several other gentlemen dismounted at the hotel door next morning and informed us that we would not go astray for at least five miles out of Fall River.

That morning ride was enjoyed by us all. The sun shone fiercely, but there were fair roads underneath us, and as the hour was shortly after 8 A. M., and we were riding over a very fair road, and riding in very pleasant company, time flew fast, and the beautiful view of the splendid sheet of water along our left, fringed for miles with green-clad hills, rich woods, and numerous thriving mill centres and hamlets, flew by us all too quickly. Five miles outside Fall River our guides left us, carrying back with them our kindly feelings for unlooked-for favors from them, and leaving with us wheelmen's wishes for an enjoyable trip.

The roadway from here on was what might be termed fair, it certainly was not good, but it was decidedly better than the experience we had be-yond Middleborough. I am anticipating, however. Our road lay through Myrickville, and the total distance to Middleborough by the route followed was something over 21 miles. A few miles outside the town, the glancing of water through the trees which bordered the roadside caught the eye of the ever-watchful Gilbert, and with the idea of a swim being within reach, he dismounted and proceeded to investigate. The result of the explora-tion was the discovery of a beautiful little sheet of water, its shore about 200 yards from the roadside, and into its cool depths the " Quartette " tumbled before you could say " Jack Robinson." The first man who found bottom thought his days were numbered. The finder of the bath and the first man in, ' fresh-water Wiese," stuck a whole foot and half a leg into what it was reasonable to suppose was mud, at any rate, his roar to the rest of us on no account to try for bottom, showed that, whatever our ex-perience of the morning had been, walking just then was not very good. The programme therefore was, dive in from the old ice slip, keep off the grass or mud, and scramble out on the end of the slip as well as you could.

One towel and two sponges were all the bath-room paraphernalia the party
had to fall back on, except the little looking-glass in Chester's handle-bar
bag, and a cake of soap in Laurie's pack, which latter we did not like to
soil the water with, as it was very clear before we went into it, and not any
perceptibly less clear when we left it, although Gilbert did try and stir up
what he said was three feet of a mud bottom. This swim put an extra edge
on our appetites, and we bore down on Middleborough for the regular mid-
day attack on the best hotel in the town.

Riding into the place we struck a cycler, who in the same breath directed us to the hotel and informed us that he was not the League Consul for the place, although he ought to have been, the fellow holding that
enviable position being of no account. This little incident set us thinking
how men were much the same all the world over. Why he should volun-
teer to us, perfect strangers and uninterested parties, the inside of things
cycling in Middleborough at a minute's notice, and berate the League offi-
cial of the place, without our having some terrible grievance to relate,
shows what sentimental nonsense in regard to cycling matters still lingers
with wheelmen. Our new friend evidently had as good an opinion of himself as he had a poor one of the other fellow.

Middleborough is not much of a place, but we got a fair dinner at, I
think, the Newmarket House.

Before leaving for Plymouth, we heard the most doleful stories of the
badness of roads leading to that place, and as long as we were going to
Boston, the universal advice was, leave Plymouth alone and go on to Boston through Taunton and the good roads of that region.

We were deaf to this advice, however. It was true that at Boston a trip
could be taken by steamer round the coast to Plymouth, but we were within
18 miles of the place, and, as Laurie said, " We'll get to the Rock, boys, to-
night, if we walk the best part of the way."

The route chosen was to the left of the direct way. Through Carver is
the shortest way from Middleborough to the coast, but if you go through
Carver you also go through sand, which although not spelled with a big
" S," on general occasions, is a bigger place than Carver to cyclers who
ride through that locality. We followed a northern course to Plympton
and North Plympton, and ran into Kingston, four miles above Plymouth
on the coast, from which place into Plymouth runs a fine stretch of macadamized road. Before reaching Kingston, owing to the solicitation of Gil,
we took a road "through the woods" recommended to us among a dozen
others by no doubt well-meaning but cruel friends. Gil is the very mischief on roads "through the woods," as some of the party on a late cycling
excursion to Washington can testify, and he "hollers," too, before he gets
out of them. On the occasion of the woods near Kingston, however, his
"hollering"—it was not singing—of popular ditties of the order of "Sweet
Violets," and inducing the rest of us to sing, did one good thing, it pre-
vented very much swearing being done, and it was just as well such was
the case, as our vocabulary in the line of "cuss words" required husband-
ing for occasional use later on.

Well, we got out of the woods—walking, mind you—and dropped right
off on a good macadamized road, which it is fair to suppose would have
been cultivating the acquaintance of our tires long before had we not
gone "walking" with Wiese through the woods. Everybody looked at
the road, and—held their peace.

While we held our peace, however, the clouds which had been gathering all day refused to hold water, and just as the pretty homes of Kingston

came into sight, down came a heavy shower, and we went out of sight in a big barn. This was our first experience of rain on the trip, and, while considering ourselves lucky, we did not relish the idea of being but four miles from our destination, and with the best piece of road struck during the day, getting its face washed to our discomfort. Moreover, was not supper ahead, and were we not hungry? An old lady who had been working around after eggs, or something in that line in the barn, volunteered the information that the rain would last all night, so donning coats, a race was made of it into Plymouth.

The road runs along the high ground overlooking Plymouth Bay, and away out to the left, standing boldly up on its promontory height, we could see the monument to Miles Standish looming through the mist. The rain moderated about a mile outside the town, and we ran in, laboring more against the disability of mud than of falling water. No decision had been made as to where we should stop, and it was just as well, for the Fall River experience was enacted over again, a League member directed us to the Central House as being the L. A. W. hotel, and then, scarcely had we turned to make for the neighborhood of supper when, a member of the Plymouth Bicycle Club came up, and in the most friendly way offered the use of the club-house to store our wheels during our stay. This offer was of course accepted, and then Charles G. Bradford and A. E. Lewis, of the Plymouth Club showed us our hotel, and left word they would see us again. This was treatment that savored of the good old days when wheelmen were few and far between, and the " wheel " was necessarily a password to good-fellowship—and, by the way, who says that the L. A. W. is of but little account? Probably only the cyclers who sit at home at ease, and who do not work for the good cause beyond cavilling at the men who do for the interests of cycling the very best they can.

While the " Quartette" dried off and had supper—and it was a good one, too, that host E. J. Shaw provided—the rain came harder than ever, and the idea of going out to sample the sights of the old Puritan town was about given up when our new friends from the Plymouth Club appeared, and informed us that we were booked to go to the Armory, where the first concert of the season would be given by the Regiment Band, and where a dance would wind up the occasion. Chester jumped at the word dance, but a blue look stole over his face as he heard the added news, " All the town will turn out, lots of pretty girls, find you all partners, no trouble." Chester's countenance was clouded, he was looking at his rubber-soled shoes. Rubber soles or no rubber soles, we went to the concert, and listened to the strains of a band that has gained more than a local celebrity under the baton of E. Thurston Damon, well-known in Boston as a leader of ability. And after the universally popular " skirt dance " had been rendered to an encore—fancy the grave Puritans of the long-ago Plymouth encoring a skirt dance—our Gil and our Chester shook a foot around the big armory with some very tangible skirts, and the writer held the caps of the party, with all the silver Keystones facing one way and toward the optics of the Plymouth brethren, on the floor and in the galleries.

Poor Chester, his prettiest young lady, whatever she may have thought of the wearer, she did not think much evidently of rubber-soled shoes, for she went out of the room on the arm of "a handsomer man !" no, on the arm of her mother. Good night, Chester.

Heroic sleepers on yon classic mound,
  That watches ever by the outer edge
Of this New World, which at your coming found
  More than a dream fulfilled, and a high pledge
Of Heaven's good-will toward man, ye reck not
  That I stand on this fair shore
And gaze with reverent awe on that which speaks
  To me, and will speak evermore
To all who owe allegiance to this land,
To all who dwell on proud Columbia's strand,
Or plain, or mount, of the great boon that ye
Wrested from fate and evil days, and placed
Free at the feet of all humanity, and graced
The records of the fuller and completer earth
With a true God-like gift, when giving birth
To a new life that throws its glorious span
Ungauged across the future lot of man.

Heroic sleepers, we your children stand
Here on the edge of our great fatherland,
And, while the breeze of this New England blows
Over yon mound, and while the great tide flows
Forward and back, on ocean's heaving breast,
Turn we from where in sweet and hallowed rest
Sleep of our country's founders, ye, the noblest and the best.

Plymouth, Mass. What associations crowd themselves on all those who take an interest in the land in which they live when the name of that little New England coast town is mentioned. To the average American a visit to Plymouth will always be interesting if he does not choose to make it instructive.

The scene of the early trials and struggles of those heroic souls who for conscience' sake left home and country and went forth to found a nation, will ever be held sacred by their descendants, now enjoying the legacy left by them, the greatest and most valuable that man can leave to man, the legacy of freedom.

It may be that those rugged old forefathers of the America of to-day did not realize the stupendous work they were inaugurating. It may be that their legacy, curiously enough, was born under auspices and had its first nurturing amid associations that were as intolerant and as undesirable as the manners and methods which had driven them to take up a work which all the world honors them now for putting their hand to without looking back. This may all be true, but no matter for the temporary working garb, the work was done and done well, and while the "Pilgrim Fathers," and the Pilgrim Mothers, too, sleep calmly on that green hill by the Massachusetts shore, their names are being handed down through the centuries as honored creators of the nation.

The rain fell heavily during the whole night of our stay in Plymouth, and for half of the next day, Wednesday. What could we do except eat as much as possible at breakfast, smoke a cigar or two, look out of the hotel windows, and wish for some religious works—we had read the papers—to while away the time. Toward 10 o'clock the rain grew lighter, and, borrowing a few umbrellas, we accepted the invitation of a Mr. H. W. Loring to go round to his club, the Plymouth Club, I think—at any rate it is the big social club of the town, to which most of the business men belong. Here, ensconced in comfortable quarters, several games of whist put us over the time until nearly noon, when our hospitable new acquaint ance wrote out an order for our admission to the Loring Co.'s tack factory, and through the mud we sallied down to see what was a most interesting sight. The making of tacks is quite an industry in Massachusetts. By this time the clouds were breaking away over toward Duxbury, and the tall column erected to the old hero, Miles Standish, commenced to stand out black against the gray sky, and the word was dinner first and the "Rock" and patriotism after. The rain had not spoiled our appetites, and, when these were satisfied, a climb to the summit of the forefathers' burying-ground, on the hill in the centre of the town, followed. Here the moldering headstones, boasting the wonderful antiquity for young America of several hundred years, were inspected, as no doubt they have been many and many times by interested pilgrims like ourselves, and then, bundles were once more strapped on machines and the journey renewed, with the historic " Rock " for our first stopping-place.

"Is that Plymouth Rock?" said Gilbert, as we rode up, dismounted, and deposited our machines at the foot of the hill rising from the place where the historic piece of stone rests under its monumental granite covering.

"That's it," said Laurie, commencing to unstrap his camera ; " what did you expect to find?"

"Why I thought it would be a big rock standing up out of the water yonder, but that's only a big stone, and it's cracked, too, and plastered up."

" Well, better have it plastered up than falling to pieces. I expect you want a ' Holy Coat of Treves ' kind of antiquity, Gilbert," said Chester.

"Look at the peanuts, boys!" suddenly cried Laurie, almost dropping his camera ; " look at them, never mind the rock and the plaster, Gil, go get some of those peanuts."

" I have not seen a peanut since I left good old Philadelphia," said Chester. And forthwith he went over to the basket man vending the precious product of American forests, and laid in a stock of the delicacy dear to the hearts and palates of the masses.

Of all the things that the writer abhors in the way of shell commodities it is peanuts. Their taste is pretty nearly as bad as their smell, when the live charcoal has squeezed out of them that which to the bulk of Philadelphia's citizens is a fragrance to which the odor of the rose of Sharon or of Childs' is as nothing. Peanuts! deliver me from them, whether they are securely bagged up in pint lots on the costermonger's tray on Market Street, or whether they are in the pocket of some belated traveler on one of the night-line cars, or whether they are reposing in the lap and busying the fingers and the facial make-up of some fair creature who has petitioned you to "Oh! do, now, get me a few peanuts, please do." Peanuts! faugh, take them away, ye degenerate members of the "Quartette." I will take instead a pretzel and a mug of Milwaukee as my portion, while I sit here and gaze on this historic stepping-stone to fame if it was not to fortune.

When we got done looking at the rock we mounted our machines and then the hill, and bidding adieu to our friends of the Plymouth Club, Messrs. Skinner, Bradford, and Lewis, proceeded on our way toward Kingston, to stop en route and view the noted Forefathers' Monument. This mass of granite stands on the top of a hill back from the town, and overlooking the waters of the harbor and the spot whereon the forefathers landed. It consists of a massive pedestal, and on it the figure of a female wrought out of granite, and facing seaward. It is said to be the largest granite statue in the world, and from its heroic pose and lonely situation, on the brow of an eminence devoid of timber, it has a weird fascination for the visitor, in keeping with the generally gray and stony landscape, and the checkered fortunes of those whose story it perpetuates. On the sides of the pedestal are representations in marble relief, covered with glass, of episodes in the dramatic story of the Pilgrim Fathers, and above these are tabulated the names of the forefathers, and of the white-winged ancient sailers of the ocean, on which they braved "the dangers of the seas."

The Forefathers' Monument was the last thing of interest we saw in Plymouth. Down the hill and along the good road into Kingston was the word, leaving on the right the memento to Miles Standish, which we had not time to travel to, and then at 4 P. M. the programme was on to Boston.

And to Boston we went, over roads that, although in Massachusetts, were none of the best for wheelmen to travel over. Through Kingston, Duxbury, Marshfield, and Hanover to Weymouth. We must have taken a rather roundabout way, for the inner man was complaining, and it was seven o'clock when we drew up at the hotel in Weymouth and demanded supper. Weymouth is a good step out of Boston, I want you to know, when you make an eight o'clock start in the evening. A 12-mile ride on Lancaster Pike after dark is all right, but into Boston through Braintree, Quincy, Neponset, and Dorchester Avenue, with its miles of belgian block pavements and its hordes of hooting gamins, is not by any means fine riding. We reached our stopping place, the United States Hotel, about 10 P. M.

As this history does not pretend to be a guide-book, little need be said about the good old city of Boston, beyond that in it we found all that we expected, and much more.

We expected to find an extraordinary amount of ultra-cult, and we found it, even to the extent of discovering a waiter at the United States Hotel who would insist upon prefacing what he considered perhaps as attentive queries with the words, "Will you gentlemen be pleased to?" etc., etc.

And we found more than the evidences of a general good education with which the inhabitants of the "Hub" are credited. We found in the harbor the "White Squadron," and our desire to see what "Uncle Sam's" pretty ships looked like tempted us to take a sail on the placid waters of Boston Harbor, and on deciding to do this, we killed two sights on the one sail, and went on to the well-known Nantasket Beach, which is to Boston what Coney Island is to New York or what Atlantic City is to Philadelphia.

When you want to go to Nantasket from Boston, if you are a stranger in the "Hub," you had better tackle one policeman after another until you find one who can direct you to Rowe's Wharf, and when you have found the well-informed "mimber of the force," you will attentively listen to him while he says, with an assumption of most intense gravity, "Yis, I'll tell yez. Yez'll be afther goin' down this next sthreet here, an' turn to the roight there, de yez see, an' thin down to the roight ag'in, an' yer roight there."

When you get your directions the trouble only begins, for you have to adhere to them strictly, or, ten chances to one, you will come right on top of the same policeman inside of ten minutes, and on tackling him the second or third time his Hibernian astuteness is aroused, and you stand a good chance of being "run in" as a suspicious character.

Our sail to Nantasket Beach was a most enjoyable one. The "White Squadron" of the United States Navy happened to be lying off the city, and a sham fight, embracing an attack on Deer Island, was on deck the day we sampled the blue waters of Boston Harbor. Hundreds of craft were out to see the evolutions of the men-of-war, and numerous excursion steamers, loaded down with people, were passed by our boat as we steamed toward the old town of Hull, en route to Nantasket.

Rowe's Wharf is named after John Rowe, who is famed as being the citizen who proposed making the first revolutionary cup of tea in Boston Harbor.

" Who knows how tea will mingle with salt water," said stout old John Rowe on December 16th, 1773, and shouts of laughter rang through the classic shadows of the Old South Church, where Boston's citizens were in meeting.

On leaving the wharf you pass first Thompson's Island, then Fort Independence, the stone walls and black guns of which the writer had not seen for over 20 years. Then you run by Spectacle Island, Long Island, the curious pile of stones known as Nix's Mate, Deer Island, Gallop's Island, Rainsford Island, and a number of other patches of land surrounded by the generally quiet waters of the harbor.

The steamer stops at the old town of Hull, once a place of importance, but now more noted as a suburban resort for Boston people than as a seaport, and shortly after you enter the winding Weir River and run up to the wharf at Nantasket Beach. The beach is on the opposite or ocean side of the neck of land on which you disembark, and immediately on setting foot ashore you are assailed by a couple of dozen " Jehus," monarchs of the lumbering coaches attached to the numerous hotels and restaurants and all offering rides free to their different hostelries, where you can get the biggest dinner, clam-bake, or otherwise for the moderate sum of 50 cents. We gave them all the cold shoulder, however, and walked across to the region of hotels, merry-go-rounds, fortune-tellers, and bathers. There were but few bathers in. It was, however, too good a chance to be missed, and inside of a few minutes Gil Wiese was once more tasting the sweets of salt water wetness. This time he was all right, and a crowd of a couple of hundred people soon assembled along the beach to watch the antics of the " Queer Quartette."

Of course we did the sights in Boston, visited Bunker Hill, the Old South Church, the historic Common, Trinity Church, Commonwealth Avenue, and the hundred and one other places of interest which this old " hotbed of sedition" boasts.

Everything went along smoothly, except that Gilbert imagined every one was looking at his shapely calves, and he felt uncomfortable, accordingly, just in proportion to the amount of admiration with which he supposed certain persons viewed his handsome nether proportions. It was useless to try and persuade him that if there was any interest awakened by our appearing on the streets of æsthetic Boston in cycling guise, he did not most certainly monopolize it all. No! he would insist upon it that he was the cynosure of all eyes, and that there was never a ballet placed upon the stage or seen off it, that created such a ripple of excitement as did Gil Wiese when he favored Tremont or Washington Streets with a sight of his muscular development encased in Quaker gray. Nothing would do but that he should get a pair of pantaloons, and all honor to well-known courteous Harry Gill, of the " United States," who took the unfortunate traveler to his room and gave him the selection from six pairs of trousers. Gil thought none of them just the thing, but chose one pair that, if hitched up as they ought to have been, or as Providence and the tailor intended them to be, would have come six inches above his shoe-tops. It can be easily understood, if not seen, therefore, that when Gilbert effaced the six inches of space at the bottom by a lowering process, the upper regions assumed a relationship that the same Providence and the tailor never designed them for ; consequently, when good old Gil walked the streets, he looked very much like an old alderman with a very young face on him, and no one would ever have taken him for a trim-built " Pennsylvania " boy. But Gilbert could not see it, because he could not see them—the " pants."

We could have spent a much longer time in Boston than we did to considerable profit, but, not being millionaires in the matter of time, which commodity, according to every accepted authority, is nothing more or less than money, it was deemed expedient to cut our visit short and seek some eminence of greater altitude than Bunker Hill Monument, somewhere outside the town from whence we might perchance get even a momentary glimpse of anything that would look like the White Mountains.

Talking of Bunker Hill, it might be incidentally mentioned that if any readers of this sketch want a taste of something unique in the line of music or noise, let them, if they ever ascend the tall column that dominates Charlestown, stick their heads, to the number of three or four, through the apertures that open into the well inside the monument and howl " Annie Laurie " with all their might.

The last view of Boston was a bird's-eye one. Ascending to the roof of the new Old Colony Trust Company's building, we gazed across the great mass of brick and mortar spread below us and over the thousands of towers, steeples, and chimneys and numberless white filmy puffs of steam, floating away into nothingness, and denoting that the great pulse of the city was beating with all its accustomed health and regularity. Over the blue waters of the harbor, with its disfigurements of old black hulks and its adornments of white-winged flyers, over the heights of Charlestown, with the tall obelisk marking the historic battle-ground on Breed's Hill, cutting clear against the sky and over distant Chelsea, which we were to pass through within an hour on our way to Lynn and Salem. The view from this great sky-scraper among the many big buildings of Boston made up for us a quartette of such experiences during various cycling trips. We had, of course, sampled the magnificent vista across two States and one great river, seen from the roof of the vast pile of marble known in Philadelphia as the Drexel Building, and gazed with admiration across the wide expanse of fair Lake Michigan, and over the wilderness of smoke and steam and seething humanity that make up Chicago, from the tower of the mass of granite known as the Auditorium Building, and also feasted our eyes, with more admiration than at any of the other places, on the glorious panorama where the city of New York joins hands with Brooklyn and Jersey City, and where the noble Hudson loses its grand identity in the embrace of old ocean ; and the Boston view from the top of her latest and most pretentious mercantile building made a fitting fourth to the other three.

A League member, resident in Chelsea, whom we met on the ferry-boat going over to that place, and to whom we got talking about roads and one thing or another, offered to go to his house and get us his Massachusetts road-book, but we showed a very neatly written bulletin of directions as far as Portsmouth, N. H., which we had obtained from Mr. A. D. Peck, who, in the office of the Pope Manufacturing Co., in Boston, is the recognized Moses in the matter of roads and routes round the " Hub," and when our Chelsea friend heard that "Peck had fixed us," he seemed to think that the road-book would be superfluous, and just then up came N. U. Walker, also from the big cycling emporium on Franklin Street, and we left Boston, therefore, under very pleasant auspices. Before going further, however, we will take the opportunity of telling any cycling traveler who may want information touching Massachusetts roads, to call when in Boston on A. D. Peck, at the Pope Manufacturing Co.'s office, and they will find a courteous gentleman and a well-informed wheelman, who, as he did for us, will only be too willing to do all he can in the way of affording any information desired.

Following directions, our road from the ferry led us out Winnisemmett Street to Everett Avenue to Woodland Cemetery, and thence through Saugus to Lynn. It was about six o'clock when we left Boston, and there was a disposition on our part to stop for supper in the "Shoe City," but knowing that Salem was not much more than an hour's ride it was decided to push on and have our evening meal in the oldest settlement of any size in New England. Through Swampscott, therefore, we went, and on the road picked up a couple of Lynn riders out for an evening spin, who took us along at a slapping pace and informed us that the good road over which we were traveling was a favorite run from Boston and Lynn. Salem is only 20 miles from Boston, and, as we debouched into the splendid wide avenue, lined with noble trees, which takes you to the business portion of the town from the Boston side, we could partly realize why it is that dwellers in this pretty place are so much attached to it. Salem was at one time of considerable importance as a port. It possessed one of the finest harbors on the Atlantic seaboard, and its merchants and traders were industrious and to a certain extent enterprising. But the more go-ahead and progressive city of Boston stepped in and drew nearly all the trade of this old place to itself, and now, while many of the citizens continue to reside in Salem they carry on business in its near-by old-time rival.

The Essex House was our destination, and, although somewhat late, supper was fixed up for us in good style and we enjoyed it after what had been a smart ride in from Boston.

With its many historical associations of colonial days, Salem would have been an interesting spot to have stopped in for a day or so, but as our destination was "beyond," an early start the next morning was agreed upon. A trip to "The Willows"—not much of a place at night—was taken, per electric cars, and on our return to the hotel we found a former Philadelphia rider, Mr. Snyder, waiting to see us. A pleasant chat with this gentleman and two or three other Salem riders filled in an hour before bed-time, and one of our new friends, Mr. Geo. E. Allen, very kindly proffered his services as guide to take us out of town the next morning.

We had arranged to do what we did not more than twice on the trip, viz., start before breakfast, and bright and early the next morning, as the clock struck half-past seven, our Salem friend appeared and the "Quartette," with their guide, turned their backs on the pretty New England town and took the road for Ipswich and breakfast. This road was a good one, and we had promise of an excellent highway all the way to Newburyport, which promise was fulfilled.

Breakfast at Ipswich put us in good form, and, bidding adieu to our obliging Salem riding companion, we struck out over the "warranted good road" to Newburyport.

This road is certainly an excellent one, and offers a great contrast to the highways which further south had been the medium of our reaching Plymouth. The road surface being first-class, the run into Newburyport, about the same distance from Ipswich that the latter is from Salem, was made ahead of dinner-time, and our ride of about 21 miles not having made us sufficiently hungry to induce a wait for the mid-day meal, forward was the word, and forward we went some 10 miles to Hampton, where a halt was called at the Whittier House. Here the proprietor, Mr. O. H. Whittier, who is, I believe, some connection of the poet, J. G. Whittier, treated us in good shape, and on the broad porch of the hotel a most comfortable lounge after dinner repaid us for waiting to satisfy the inner man in so pretty a place. The camera did good service here in catching an old stage-coach and a farmer's wagon with a team of oxen, as well as a bevy of fair tennis players who were making things lively on the courts next the house. According to advice from parties staying at the hotel, we determined to strike off to the coast, not more than a few miles distant to the right, and see Rye Beach and whatever of interest was thereabouts. Before leaving the hotel, however, and while sitting on the porch, after the two cameras had been made to capture the surrounding vistas, an amusing incident occurred. Chester had picked up an old, tattered copy of the New York *Herald* and was lazily picking out scraps of reading, when suddenly he gave vent to what was a young shout, and called to Wiese, who was enjoying a cigarette at the other end of the porch.

"Hallo! Gil," he shouted, "they've got you in the New York *Herald*. What do you think of that?"

"What do you mean? where did they hear about us?" said Gil, coming over.

"Us! I didn't say us," said Chester. "I said you; here you are as large as life, and such a description. I'll keep this paper if I have to steal it from the house here. Listen, Laurie, haven't they got Gil down fine in 'Gotham?'" And forthwith Chester, who could hardly read for laughing, gave us the following, and it was a study to watch Gilbert's face while the verse was being read.

> He came from somewhere inland,
>   From Pittsburgh, I surmise,
> And down along the Jersey coast
>   He strayed with bulging eyes;
> He saw the dainty maidens
>   Among the wavelets slosh.
> And when at last he oped his mouth
>   He simply said, "Begosh!"
>                         —*New York Herald.*

A roar of laughter all round greeted the above, and the paper was carefully put away by Chester, who thought he had got one in on Gil, who was never tired of teasing him as to his methodical tying-up of bundles and taking up time, whether in the matter of getting up in the morning or getting on his wheel after a meal.

# CHAPTER V.

Blue is the ether and blue is the sea,
Brushing the wave-tops winds blow free,
Sunshine is slanting on sails afar,
Tacking for Portsmouth's Harbor bar.
Away in the east the "Shoals" lie low,
Like a cloud too timid its face to show,
You can see the rise of the land no more
From the ragged back of the "Little Boar;"
  And you wish that you knew
  All the tales that to you
When you stood on that bluff,
  The bold winds blew
From the "Shoals" away off shore.

Leaving the village of Hampton, the road we followed led us to Hampton Beach, a fine stretch of open coast, and quite a resort for bathing and all-round sea-shore pleasures, without the assistance of Coney Island's conventional attractions. The same may be said of Rye Beach, further on, and to reach which we had to go back on our tracks and travel by way of Little Boar's Head.

Though it has a large name, this is a small place, but it is an exceedingly pretty one. We were now on the New Hampshire coast, and, as the road suddenly took a bend to the left and disclosed to us an unbroken view of the great blue ocean, stretching miles and miles outward and to left and right, a simultaneous shout went up from and a dismount was made by us all. The many beautiful residences which make up the town or hamlet of Little Boar's Head are all situated on high ground, overlooking the sea, with a wealth of green sward and trees round and back of them. Away below the waves roll lazily and curl round the rocks in wavy masses of foam, except when they dash and roar with all the force born of their ocean vantage, urged on by angry winds from seaward. Everything was serene and beautiful, however, when we paused to admire the grand vista of rock and water. Never was sea more blue. Talk of your Mediterranean skies and sea, they are equalled and surpassed by what we have on this side of the Atlantic.

Allowing the machines to rest against the fence, the four of us climbed over and lay along the brow of the bluff overlooking the water. Away out to sea and to the left could be seen the Isle of Shoals, famous as a summer resort. Several islands make up "The Shoals," and steamers ply the distance between them and the mainland, about 10 miles, several times a day. It was not without great reluctance we left so charming a spot. Accustomed to the low-lying sandy shores of New Jersey, it was a rare treat to find ourselves on a veritable rocky coast, and the little taste we were getting of it, recalling old times to at least some of us, made strong the longing for even the least little taste of the rugged shores of Maine. Gilbert, of course, had never seen anything like it, and as we lay looking out to sea, under the blue sky and the warm sunlight, his thoroughly unbiased judgment was summed up in the remark :

"Well, boys, you may talk about your ' Coney Islands,' ' Nantaskets,' or Atlantic Cities, but give me some place like this. I could live here for two weeks without any trouble."

24

" Yes, if somebody else were here too, Gil. In which case you might stay two weeks and a half or longer," said Laurie.

" What time is it, Gil?" queried Chester.

" It's just five," replied Gilbert, consulting his watch.

" Then it's time to start. I thought you would like a *reminder*, Gil," and Chester looked what might be termed a smile at the balance of the quartette, while Gilbert looked again at the dial of his time-piece, at least that is what he appeared to look at. Chester told us afterward that when he wanted to put Gil in a good humor he always asked him what time it was, and as we had noticed that there was a picture of some sort or other in the said watch, we gave Chester credit for a *finesse* that before then we did not know he possessed.

The roads round this region are simply superb, both as to surface and location. The surface is macadam, and good macadam, too, and round Little Boar's Head and Rye Beach they lead you a trip in full view of old ocean, and yet in close proximity to all that makes country life amid green fields and trees so enjoyable. One of the finest hotels in the way of a summer resort that we struck on our trip was the Farragut House at Rye Beach. Superb in its appointments, both in-door and out-door, by general consent the " Quartette," only for what was "beyond" would have liked to have settled down for a couple of weeks' stay at this grand old house, with its charms of country and seashore, its pleasures of the ball-room and tennis court and coaching roads thrown so luxuriously and lavishly together. But the Farragut House, with its charms of location and society was not meant for us, as long as we were bound for the White Mountains and " beyond," and we lingered but a short time underneath the grand old trees that make the place look like one of the ancestral halls of the England of long ago. Making a tour of the grounds, we struck out once more on the high road to Portsmouth, and passing a couple of fashionable rigs with tanned city beauties holding the reins, returning to the hotel from town, the " Quartette " were soon in the middle of the pretty old town of Portsmouth.

That the town of Portsmouth is old is a matter of history, that it is pretty is a matter of opinion. It certainly has many fine residences, very fair road surfaces, several large industrial establishments, and one of its hotels, the Rockingham, looks as though it had been taken from among palatial companions in Boston, New York, or Philadelphia and set down as a luxurious curiosity in what by comparison is a most unpretentious city.

Gilbert had not to hunt far for his " Delmonico's " or Laurie for his " Boldt's." By universal consent we were directed to the Rockingham, and on arriving there found that supper was one of the things the management paid special attention to. We had ridden altogether, since leaving Salem that morning, a distance of 62 miles, so the good meal set before us was not by any means treated with neglect. Having several friends in town, the writer proceeded to hunt them up after supper, and, having discharged this duty, returned to the hotel to find Mr. Charles A. Hazlitt, one of the jolly good old-timers of cycling, waiting to see the party. There is not a better informed cyclist in New Hampshire than Mr. Hazlitt, and on understanding that we were on an extended trip, it was his great desire that we should stop over at Portsmouth for a day or so, and see what he called some of the most interesting sights in New England. On our telling him that we could not possibly stay longer than half the following day, Sunday, he was greatly disappointed, but most kindly offered to wake us up

4

early the next morning and show us all of Portsmouth that could be seen in half a day. It was early next morning when, true to his promise, Mr. Hazlitt turned up at the hotel, and a few minutes' time saw us mounted and pedalling toward the Piscataqua River, to cross over to Newcastle. This was one of the most pleasing experiences of our trip. As an authority on the historical data connected with the neighborhood in which he lives, and as an active wheelman, conversant with the highways and byways leading to and from every point of interest, Mr. Hazlitt is a prize which the cycling visitor to Portsmouth may count himself as a spoiled child of fortune if he captures. Old Fort Constitution, with its curious gateway, about the only specimen of the portcullis feature of fortification to be seen in this northern country, the heavy black guns lying grim and sullen on the sward outside the walls, the few pyramids of shells, with grass and weeds of all kinds growing at will around and over all, struck us as being one of the most interesting things we had seen on our pilgrimage. Chester climbed to the top of the old Martello tower near the entrance. Gilbert smoked a cigarette, and asked an old ship captain who was standing by how it was that while there was no license in Portsmouth, whisky was sold to citizens and also to strangers.

" Because we likes to buy it," laconically answered the old tar. Laurie got both cameras to work, while the writer sat down on a mammoth pile of granite, cut long ago to build the new fort, but never used, and scribbled on the back of the last letter to hand from Philadelphia, a Portsmouth sentiment to carry back to the " Quaker City " :

> Useless now the embattled wall,
> The grim portcullis and the high-thrown mound,
>   All destined once to see the grim death-play
> Of strife twixt man and man ;
>   All labor spent is vain and useless now ; but stay !
> Say not quite useless, since we can
> See in these serried ranks of quarried stone,
> See in these old-time shells that here alone
> Live on, the thought that, what in hate began
> Between two peoples through whose veins there ran
> The same rich blood, may end in sovereign love
> As fixed and sure as are the heavens above.

From the top of the Martello tower Chester called to us. He was taking in the view through the agency of a field-glass which the before-mentioned old sailor carried, who was also on top of the tower. Laurie's photographs were by this time taken, and we all scrambled to the top of the squat-looking edifice that dominates the knoll of ground back of the fort. The term Martello comes from a place of that name in Corsica, where one of these small defences made a memorable resistance to attack during the French wars at the end of the last century. The visitor to Ireland can count hundreds of these towers round the coast of that island, built by orders of the British War Office, with the double object of affording work to the peasantry and providing against a threatened invasion of the country by the first Napoleon. It was a similar exigency that called into existence the circular pile of brick which, though now dismantled, watches over the waters at Portsmouth.

From the front porch of the splendid Wentworth house you can obtain a beautiful view seaward, looking toward the Isle of Shoals, and from the rear porch another view almost equally fine can be had of the river, town, country, and the faraway mountains. To these latter our gaze wandered whenever it got the chance. They, or those back of them, were the goal of our expectations, and, notwithstanding the enjoyment of the present, we could not help speculating as to what, both in the way of pleasure and pain, was in store for us.

From the rear porch of the Wentworth, our guide pointed out to us the old Wentworth Mansion, the home of Governor Wentworth. As every State has its more or less noted Governors, so has New Hampshire, and in early colonial days the name of Governor Benning Wentworth, as it is still, was identified prominently with New Hampshire and with Portsmouth. The story of his marriage to Martha Hilton is a romantic incident that possessed so much of interest as to inspire Longfellow to pen one of his prettiest verse narratives.

Crossing the long bridge from the island over to Portsmouth we got a distant view of the Kittery Navy Yard and the old frigate " Constitution," which lies there, an object of patriotic veneration to all good citizens who have attended public school and profited thereby. A ride around the town and an inspection of what it had to show in the way of residences put us well on to dinner-time, and, as our departure was scheduled for immediately after that meal, our more than kind guide bade us adieu and carried away with him our more than thanks.

And now we were to turn our backs upon the coast ; for comparatively level riding over what, for the past few days, had been good roads, we were to exchange mountain climbing and, by all accounts, indifferent highways. No matter, we were in for it and we turned our backs on the ocean and on Portsmouth with but one regret—that we had not at least a week to spend among friends and scenes alike pleasant and instructive.

It was nearly three o'clock before we got started. Our first stopping place would be Dover, and then Rochester for supper and to stay overnight. The latter place is about 20 miles from Portsmouth. A fair road carried us to Dover, though in places the ruts asserted themselves to a greater extent than was pleasant. Beyond Dover this was even more the case, and we began to think that, if the New Hampshire public highways deteriorated much more, we were in for the reverse of what is generally known as a " soft snap." However, Rochester was made all right, but not quite as early as we expected, consequently, our opportunity to see much of the place was limited, as supper had to be discussed, and then a rest on the porch with heels in air and a cigar and stories to the fore made loafing at the hotel preferable to rambling round city streets, of which we get plenty and enough when not traveling in quartettes.

Before turning in, it was agreed that the opinion of some local cycler should, if possible, be secured as to the best route to follow in entering the mountains, and as Mr. Charles Corson was known by reputation to nearly all of us, his address was secured, and, in our dreams that night we each and all of us saw ourselves coasting Mount Washington, photographing the " Profile " and " Fabyan's," blowing cigarette smoke into the face of the " Old Man of the Mountains," or dancing with pretty girls stranded in the same mountains.

# CHAPTER VI.

## LAKE WINNEPESAUKEE AND BEYOND.

### I.

When Heaven first looked on earth and threw
　A loving smile upon it,
Of all the spots that tried to gain
　That smile, but one spot won it ;
For when New Hampshire spread abroad
　Her cloud-gloved hands above her,
How could the great and mighty One
　Who made her, fail to love her.

　　O Winnepesaukee ! fairest lake,
　　　Heaven smiling o'er thy mother,
　　Brought thee to life since when it has
　　　Not smiled on such another.

### II.

As sweep ng o'er thy tide I see
　That great smile mirrored in it,
Well guarded by those grand old hills
　Which helped New Hampshire win it ;
I see the green-garbed isles lie like
　Fair gems in silver setting,
And harken to the breeze-borne song
　Of wave on rockland fretting.

　　O Winnepesaukee ! fairest lake,
　　　No other smile shall smother,
　　This smile of thine, for Heaven will ne'er
　　　Vouchsafe earth such another.

The morning of Monday broke clear and beautiful, and as it wore on also grew hot. Our original intention was to go into and through the mountains by way of North Conway, and when in Boston, the writer, growing tired of carrying a valise on his machine, packed in it everything not absolutely essential to comfort—extra films for the cameras, etc.—and shipped it on to North Conway. When, however, at an early hour on Monday morning, the Quartette walked into Mr. Corson's establishment, where he handles all kinds of bicycles and cycling goods, and, introducing themselves, asked for directions, the whole programme was changed, and, per that gentleman's advice, we switched our ideas and line of travel to the left, and decided to make a break for water ; in other words, we determined to sample the charms of New Hampshire's most beautiful lakes. Lake Winnepesaukee and the big and little Squam Lakes are known to all those who travel on this continent in search of the beautiful, and, profiting by the directions of our Rochester friend, we started at a good round pace for Farmington, New Durham, Alton, and Lake Winnepesaukee.

Getting our bearings from Mr. Corson, who had made frequent trips into the White Mountains, not all cycling trips, however, we bade adieu to Rochester and took the road to Farmington, some seven miles distant.

The riding was not what would be called first-class, but taking it all in all, it was not wholly and aggravatingly bad, as we had been led to expect it would be by dwellers east of Rochester. Rochester and Farmington people seemed to think their highways first-class, but they very evidently did not do much riding in the neighborhood of Portsmouth and Rye Beach, or they would have criticized their own road-surfaces a little more accurately. Taking the New Hampshire roads as a whole, however, through the region we traversed, they afforded good riding for Safety bicycles.

Farmington was reached about half an hour later than we had calculated, and learning from local riders that we would have to reach Alton Bay, some 11 miles distant, on Lake Winnepesaukee, by 12 o'clock, or, failing that hour, 4 o'clock P. M. in order to cross it, a start was at once made with the idea of reaching there by noon. A couple of Farmington riders taking a spin on the main street very kindly volunteered to go a piece of the way with the "Quartette," and we had the pleasure of their company for about two and a half miles out of town when they left us, and about the same time the good road also left us, or rather we left it, for from there on through New Durham there was a wealth of ruts, and once or twice the recommendation of our Farmington friends to take the train at New Durham in order to reach Alton Bay by noon came very near being entertained by the sun-roasted four. The day was a boiling hot one, and not by any means the kind of day to tempt over-exertion on the part of cycling tourists, so the very wise conclusion was reached, at a council of war held in a dry water-course, flanked by a luxurious growth of ripe raspberries, to take things easy, take a pull at the raspberries and at something else to head off evil consequences from a hearty indulgence in the tempting fruit, take dinner at Alton Bay, take the 4 o'clock trip across the lake, and perhaps take supper at Centre Harbor or some place beyond, on the further side of the lake. This pleased all parties, and after a grand loaf in the shady, dried-up water-course, the road was again tackled, and about 12.30 the houses of Alton came into view. The first thought on our reaching the town was, of course, dinner.

No! I am wrong. Perhaps the first thought was—well! is this place prohibition also. If this was not the first thought, as well as the writer can remember, it was the first expression that fell from the lips of one of the party—who shall be nameless—on catching sight of the hospitable roof of G. F. Savage's hotel.

Whether the place is prohibition or not, readers can find out for themselves when they visit it, at all events, if good treatment and good food is a desideratum, by all means look up Mr. G. F. Savage.

And now a noteworthy incident has to be chronicled. Up to this point of the pilgrimage, our Laurie had manfully borne the disability which the ownership of whiskers seemed to impose upon him, while traveling through the frequented and unfrequented beauty spots of New England. While enjoying a half hour's rest on the hotel porch before dinner, suddenly, our knight of the camera jumped from his chair and said :

" Boys, I'll do it !"

" Do what ?" asked Gilbert.

" Get shaved," was the brief if it was not the witty answer.

" Look out, Chester, we'll have another ' Richmond in the field,' as far as the ladies are concerned, by the time we reach the White Mountain notches," remarked Weise.

" I'm satisfied you're handicapped just twice as much as before, Gil," replied the good-humored Chester, and Gilbert forthwith busied himself fishing a last cigarette from a dilapidated box.

Twenty minutes elapsed, and just as dinner was announced back came our fraternal fourth party, minus the masculine embellishment of a carefully cultivated beard, in the full enjoyment of which he had but lately left us. Gilbert, who had never seen his traveling companion clean shaven before, nearly succumbed to extreme surprise and perhaps a little envy, for by general consent, the three-quarters of the quartette who had not been to the "barber of Alton," voted that a good-looking individual had been added to the party. It may be noted in passing that it seemed as though with the loss of his hirsute facial appendages, our fellow-traveler seemed to have effected a clear gain in the line of eating capacity, and this characteristic followed him throughout the remainder of the trip.

It is but a short mile from Alton to Alton Bay, the point of embarkation for the further end of beautiful Lake Winnipesaukee. It is at this point that the Concord & Montreal Railroad makes connection with the handsome steamers that ply on the lake, and which transport visitors to the numerous pleasure resorts on its profusely indented and well-wooded shores.

Ahead of time, we lay about the wharf watching the small fish and some snapping-turtles enjoying themselves round the piles in the beautiful clear water below the jetty. Here a telegram was sent on to North Conway, to have the writer's "grip" forwarded to Bethlehem, which telegram miscarried, entailing some little uneasiness among the party later on, relative to the matters of fresh films for the camera, and fresh fittings in the way of clothes for the writer.

By and by, round the far side of the green island half a mile from port, could be seen creeping the smokestacks of the expected steamer, looking, as Gilbert remarked, much as they would look from certain points of view on the Mississippi, and in a few minutes, round the end of the island came the "Mount Washington," the handsome boat that was to convey us to the other end of the lake, about 23 miles distant. From the moment of setting foot on deck of this well-appointed steamer, the real enjoyment of the trip in the way of novelty commenced. Whether this was in part owing to the discovery that we would not be charged for the carriage of our wheels, I will not say. I do not think, however, that any such mercenary motive for our indulging in light hearts could have existed ; we were above it, as much above such feelings as were the high hills around us above the fair bosom of the beautiful sheet of water over which we were swiftly and yet gently speeding.

There were the usual adieus, handshaking, wavings, etc., to other travelers left on the wharf, and then every one settled down to the enjoyment of a ride alike restful and beautiful.

Why do not more of our great commonality sample pleasures such as the one under notice, which are as easily attainable as many which command and receive an amount of attention and patronage they do not, comparatively speaking, deserve? Instead of spending a certain amount of time and money on pleasures more or less connected with every-day city life, it would seem as though, at the expense of a little patience—you can hardly say self-denial—and by a judicious use of capital, more of our people could, in a week, or two or three, taken from the 52 which make up the year, learn something of the magnificent land that lies around them. If not in an extended way, at least in a local way, this could be done, and right here the bicycle comes in as an agent, the best of any, perhaps, placed at the disposal of the ordinary run of every-day workers. Get your bicycle, and it will lead you to learn something, be it much or little, about your country.

Steadily swept the "Mount Washington" over the bright, sparkling waters of Winnepesaukee. It was a glorious sail. The day was superb, a trifle too hot, perhaps, but we were not on a rutty road, we were on a well-appointed steamboat, gliding over a sea of blue and silver. Rattle-snake Island was passed on our left, and, as we progressed, island after island, bay after bay, hill after hill, and mountain after mountain was either passed or came into view and was then shut out again by some new object of interest. The different-hued foliage on the many hills inclosing the lake lent a charm to the panorama flying by that was as ever-interest-ing as it was ever-changing. Islands with small summer residences on them, boats lying in little coves, odd fishermen dominating solitary rocks, other islands with white tents pitched under green canopies, where camp-ing parties were thanking Heaven before meals, or swearing at the cook after them; great mountains in the distance, and beyond them—what? Well! we did not know. All these and many other sights which make Winnepesaukee all that it is said to be, with its 300 islands, its waters of crystal, and its waves of silver, its sky, when we saw it, as blue as its hills were green; all these and many other beauties made us sorry when our boat ran into the wharf at Centre Harbor, and we had to decide whether we would stop at the Senter House that night or seek a lodging further on. We decided to go on. There was still an hour and a half of daylight, and although we were ignorant as to hotel accommodations ahead, we de-termined to risk the chances of having to sleep in the woods. Mr. Corson had given us the name of a large boarding-house, about a mile outside the town, where it would be preferable to stop, in view of the fact that the said mile lay up, as John Bunyan might have written it, a very steep and terrible hill. We had heard of this hill from two riders whom we had met on the other side of the lake, they having ridden down it. We walked up it, and after walking up failed to find our promised stopping-place. What to do was the question. Tackle the Sturtevant House, half a mile on, was Laurie's suggestion. This is an old farm-house turned into a mountain boarding-house, and right comfortable it looked, sitting on the elevation it occupies over the road. Full up, no accommodations, go back about a mile and a half to Centre Harbor, or else go on some five miles to the Asquam House, was the word here. Go back down that long, long hill. Oh! no; better go on if we have to walk every step of the way in the dark. Our decision was looked at with wonder by a couple of ladies and three city wearers of red and black blazers, just out from having had supper, and I doubt not but that some talk was indulged in after we de-parted touching the recklessness of "those bicycle riders." In half a minute's time the "Quartette" was congratulating itself upon its bravery in pushing ahead, for a long down-grade, rough as they make them, sent machines and jaws rattling, and also sent our spirits up to high-water mark. We must have run down a full mile before bringing up to push on the pedals once more.

> "Steady, boys, steady, ready, boys, ready,
> Duty, boys, duty, wherever you are sent;
> Never know defeat, boys, death before retreat, boys,
> That is the song of our Regiment."

So sang Gil Wiese for the hundredth time, as we commenced to pay up for our pleasureable down-grade run. It was now dusk, and we had as much as we could do to keep on the machines. Indeed, we could not keep on them; it was ride, boys, ride, and then walk, boys, walk, and then again slide, boys, slide, ere we could clap the brake on to prevent going down grade faster than was quite agreeable. At a fork of the road we nearly went wrong, but, fortunately, a solitary cottage farm-house stood right at the junction point, and though a pretty 15-year-old country lass could not tell us much about the route, an old man, who, in point of looks, was the greatest contrast to such a child that I think I ever saw, pointed out our road to the Asquam House. Up to the present we had not learned that this mountain hostelry stood on Shepard's Hill, boasting an elevation of 800 feet.

It was ticklish riding now, and once again we nearly lost our way, but a ten minutes' hunt for an inhabited house, saved us from journeying off to Plymouth. There are but few houses round this region, and several of the ones we did see were untenanted.

When about a mile and a half from our destination, we came upon an extensive farm establishment, in front of which stood an old man, as venerable looking as the place itself. He was hale and hearty, however, and on our stopping to ask directions, he put a number of questions to us as to who we were and where going.

Wiese almost floored him at the first go off, by telling him we were from Philadelphia. "You don't mean to tell me," said he, "you've ridden those things from Philadelphia." "The best part of the way, except across the water," replied Gil.

A rather strong expression followed from the old countryman which he followed up with : "Philadelphia is a great place. Was there once goin' to the war. We thought they treated us well in Boston, but when we got to Philadelphia, I'll never forget it. Nothin' was too good for us. I never saw Philadelphia since, and don't suppose I ever shall again, but there's lots of us yet thinks there's no city like that of yours."

He spoke so earnestly about the kindness of Philadelphia people that we spent ten full minutes chatting to him, before asking all we wanted to know. In answer to our query as to whether we had much of a hill to go up to the Asquam House, he stuck his thumbs into his suspenders and broke out with :

"Hills, hills is it? You've got a mountain to go up, a ——— of a big mountain, the biggest one you've seen yet. But, come now, you don't mean to say you are going up on those bicycles?"

We assured him that we purposed so doing, and after an expression of sorrow on his part that he could not put us up for the night, we went on for our mile and a half jaunt to the Asquam House. It was very well that we were not cognizant of all that was before us, for I question whether we would have had the courage to climb the tremendous hill to the house that night if we had known what the task would be like. There was no sing to Gil Wiese when we got to the top, and saw the "lights of home" on our right, up a further incline. Chester said he had pretty nearly enough of the mountains already. Laurie said nothing, but no doubt he thought much, and wished himself at home on Arch Street, Philadelphia, and the writer wondered if he would have sufficient wit to say his prayers, provided he got some supper before having to perform that duty. Mr. Cilly, the well-known proprietor of the "Asquam," fixed us all right, however, and probably he never had four more played-out travelers in need of food and lodging than the "Quartette" who that night tumbled into the Asquam House.

# CHAPTER VII.

## FROM THE BIG AND LITTLE SQUAM TO THE FRANCONIA NOTCH.

### SQUAM LAKE.

Beautiful lake of the mountain world,
    Resting in shadows deep.
Beautiful lake of a beautiful land
    Round thee the hill-tops keep
Ever their watch, that the wind-god may
    Breathe but a sigh o'er thy sleep.

Beautiful lake is this greater Squam,
    Veiling its isle-flecked face
Under the woodland's cloak flung out
    To soften the rough embrace.
Of the hills that make this greater Squam
    Of rest, the abiding place.

The sunlight was streaming in through our windows on our awakening the next morning.  By this it need not be supposed that the "Quartette" were late in rising, for it will be remembered that the time of year was July, and also we were on the top of a very high hill, which latter fact, owing to the experience of the previous evening, we were fully cognizant of.  What a grand prospect greeted our eyes on leaving our rooms and exchanging their narrow limits for the broad freedom of the porch running round the hotel.  On almost every side a panorama of mountain and lake greets the eye, and we found but few if any views on our trip that came up, in the way of serene loveliness, to the view on Squam Lake from the Asquam House.  Away below us was more than a semicircle of water, extending round the eminence on which this splendid summering place is situated. The greater and lesser Squam Lakes stretch around the base of Shepard's Hill, the surface of the former dotted with many islands, and both surrounded by ranges of hills that inclose their waters and notably in the case of the larger lake, give them a beauty that perhaps can be matched by but few such places either in the Old World or the New.  Among the smaller lakes of America, Squam Lake, it is said, occupies a first place, and I am willing to believe the statement, for certainly I never saw a more beautiful combination of water, wood and mountain within small compass than where the "Big Squam" lies in quiet content amid the retirement of the New Hampshire hills.

It had been our intention to leave early, immediately after breakfast, in fact, but, when a good meal had made us feel the least little bit lazy, and when the spirit of rest which seemed to dominate the whole place and permeate the air took hold of us, the programme was changed and the time of starting postponed until after dinner.  There were a great many guests at the house, and the numerous pretty cottages on the slope of the hill overlooking the lake were almost all full of rest-seeking families. About 200 yards from the hotel and standing on the brow of the hill are two or three pine trees, and it is under these trees that the poet Whittier loves to sit and look out over a vista that coaxed from his pen his well-known lines on this beautiful spot.

5                                                    33

"I'm going to make a motion," said Gilbert, as we took in the charming view from near the Whittier trees. "I move that we stay here instead of going on among those mountains."

"I second the motion," the writer ventured to remark, but Laurie looked at us reproachfully as he adjusted the lens of his camera to capture the physiognomy of the beautiful sheet of water below us.

"We did not start out to loaf around Newport, Squam Lake, or any other place," put in Chester. "The fact is," he continued, "Gil, here, saw a couple of extremely pretty girls, from down South somewhere, on the porch last night, and he wants to stay here, and make their acquaintance."

"You would be a good hand to write novels, Chester; you've got a capital imagination," said Gilbert, having recourse to his cigarette box.

"Well, it's true," said Chester, putting that peculiar high emphasis on the word true, which is characteristic of voices not cut out for bass singing.

"Well, have it so ; don't you want to stop, too ? Look at that lake there. I'm going down for a swim directly, perhaps a row, too. Look at those mountains. We've got as good or better out Pittsburgh way ; but, still, these are all right ; think of the breakfast we had—no scrapping around and worrying to find a decent place to get a meal at. Now, I think if we are wise travelers we will lay up here ; honest, now, I mean it."

And Gil really did mean what he said, and, "but small blame to him," as the Irishman said, for wishing to take it easy under circumstances and amid associations as pleasant as those of Squam Lake and the Asquam House.

Very shortly after breakfast we started down the hill and brought up at the boat-house, from which place we were rowed over to the bath-houses by the keeper of the boats, who turned out to be a student from one of the New England colleges putting in his vacation in that fashion. We found among the waiters at the hotel several other students who were spending their vacation making an honest penny in that capacity, and, doubtless, benefiting by the change of occupation and by the health-giving properties of the place. At the bath-houses, owing to the kindness of a couple of the guests, we secured bathing-suits and took a swim in the clear, cool waters of the lake. It is surprising how clear the water in these New Hampshire lakes is. You can see very often a distance of 20 feet and more to the pebbly bottom. In Squam Lake there are large quantities of fish, and fishing parties are one of the institutions of the place.

It was 3 o'clock in the afternoon when, fortified by dinner and a rest of about three-quarters of an hour after it, the "Quartette" mounted machines once more, and in a whirlwind of dust rushed down Shepard's Hill, round the shore of the Lake, and followed the road in the direction of Plymouth. According to advice, we left this road after traveling a short distance and took one to the right, which led us over, perhaps, a more hilly route, but which carried us away from sand, which we understood was a feature of the road near Plymouth. Our object was to strike over to the Pemigewasset River by way of Livermore Falls, and then follow the road along this stream by way of Campton, Thornton, and Woodstock into the Franconia Mountains. The road was a very fair one ; indeed, so far we could not complain on the head of roads, as we had been favored with good ones on the whole, and better than we had expected to find. At Livermore Falls, which we reached by dint of many inquiries, the river is spanned by a high iron bridge, and from this bridge a charming view is had of the falls, which, while not very large, are extremely picturesque, as the water rushes over huge, jagged masses of rock. Crossing the stream, we followed the road leading along the west bank, and just as supper-time was well-nigh vanished, and with it, of course, supper, the tree-covered hostelry known as Sanborn's came into view, and it was resolved that enough had been done for that day, and that a stop over for the night at Sanborn's was the proper thing. This well-known stopping-place for visitors to the New Hampshire hill country stands on the road running through to the Franconia Notch, and, with its annex on the opposite side of the same road, is quite a large place. Although somewhat late, supper was not long in making its appearance, and seeing that we had covered some 12 miles during the afternoon, the meal was extremely welcome. After supper there was a long sit on the porch, a smoke, and some chatting with the other guests, and then an invitation to join a progressive euchre party at the annex. There was only room for two, and the lucky two were Chester and the writer, so Gilbert and Laurie sat on the porch, and while Gil smoked, the fourth party to the "Quartette" told him that there were 16 ladies in the party in the large room, where the bell tinkled and chairs were pushed backward and vacated and occupied again by fortunate or unfortunate players. The two non-players went over after a while and passed the time on the main hotel porch, while other players than their traveling-companions won the prizes at the euchre party.

"Serves you right; you need not have expected to win after leaving us the way you did," said Laurie, on our return.

Leaving Sanborn's the next morning we determined that, as during the past few days loafing rather than riding had been the programme, we would bestir ourselves and get over some ground. The intention was all right, but the matter of putting it into execution was a little bit difficult. In the first place it was hard work, very hard work, riding. The road-surface was fair, to be sure, but the grades were a little too much for comfort, and it was a remarkable fact that the four minds of the "Quartette" seemed very often to run in the same channel, and nobody just around that neighborhood had the hardihood to dispute the fact that the "walking was very good." And then again, the magnificent scenery cropping up on either hand as we closed in on Woodstock, the giant mountains looming up near by and in the distance the leaping, tumbling, laughing, and always lovely Pemigewasset River, the necessity for catching and carrying away with us some of the glorious scenes we were passing through, all these had an influence in keeping us from making fast time, and it was not until on the far side of Woodstock that lowering clouds and distant peals of thunder sent us into North Woodstock for dinner at a faster rate than we had ridden for days.

It was a question after dinner whether to go on or not. A heavy shower had fallen over North Woodstock just before we reached it; the mountains were covered with fast-flying clouds, which rolled along their sides in great white masses, and the mutterings of the distant thunder made subdued music through the hills. We had stopped at the Russell House, and from the plateau back of it were shown by another traveler the towering masses of hills ahead of us, through which we were about to penetrate. As it was evident that we would have rain, whether we remained at North Woodstock or pushed on, a forward movement was decided upon, and the road through the Franconia Notch, by way of the Flume House and the Profile, was taken, with some misgiving as to the probability of reaching either place ahead of rain. The Profile House was about 10 miles distant.

It was on this portion of the road that we ran across one of the prettiest little cascades we had dropped on in our travels. It is known among the many others along the line of the beautiful Pemigewasset as the Cascade in the Franconia Notch, and on one of the large flat boulders underneath the fall of water is to be seen a good representation of a gigantic footprint. This is said to be a relic of the Old Man of the Mountain, or, if you choose so to consider it, it is a legacy left by the "Old Boy" himself from the time when he used to go rampaging around, the monarch of all he surveyed in these magnificent wilds.

The first thing Gil Wiese did was to jump all over the holy or unholy imprint, and the writer never knew he was on sacred rock until after he had lain all over it to reach down for a drink, having his legs held by two others of the party, for fear of his making too close acquaintance with the pool. Beneath the rock over which the water plunges, is a deep pool, which must at least be 30 feet in depth, hollowed out by the unceasing flow of the beautiful clear water through ages. You can see to the bottom without the least difficulty, the water being as clear as the proverbial crystal. Both above and below this beauty-spot of the Pemigewasset the stream forces its way through little cañons and over hundreds of rocks, and forms countless little cascades that throw the music of their waters upon the ear of the traveler as he follows the road through the famed Franconia Notch.

Bright Pemigewasset, sweet stream of the hills,
  Thy free, bounding waters are foaming,
O'er rock and through fissure, as slowly we force
  Our way through the Notch in the gloaming;
The Flume is before us, thy music behind,
  It drops but at times on our hearing,
And fainter still grows the last plaint of thy song,
  For thy beautiful birthplace we're nearing.

Bright Pemigewassett, sweet stream, I will tell
  Thy story wherever I wander,
As breeze borne across the dark valley it comes
  From thy rock-girdled banks over yonder;
I hear it and love it ; the story is this,
  That one of New England's fair daughters
Lost her voice in the hills, and 'twas found there by thee,
  And lives on in thy musical waters.

The Pemigewasset River rises in the beautiful sheet of water known as Profile Lake, and runs through the enchanting valley that takes its name from it, and up which, for some 20 miles, we had been traveling. We were now fairly among the mountains. For several miles the other side of Woodstock the cameras had seen hard service, and many were the views caught and stored away in the little black boxes on the handle-bars of the machines. All the day, from the time we left Sanborn's, successions of hills came into view, each rising higher than the other, then larger mountains loomed up through the gaps in the lower hills and across the intervales, and still we kept climbing, climbing until the hills became mountains all round, and we landed, as before remarked, in North Woodstock for dinner, and then passed on up the road through the Franconia Notch. The railroad ends at North Woodstock, and from there on to the Profile House all travel is carried on by stage-coach, a number of which ancient equipages we saw while in the mountains. Shortly after leaving Woodstock we caught up with and passed one of these lumbering six-horse coaches. It was loaded with people, satchels, boxes, and trunks, and the horses had a hard pull. The professional tooling it, did not like the idea of us passing him, and kept us pocketed in the narrow roadway for nearly a quarter of a mile, but a level stretch a little wider than the general run of roadway gave us the desired chance, and we bade him good-bye. We made as good time as he did, notwithstanding the heavy grades, and reached the Lake ahead of him.

Profile Lake lies directly off the road to the left before you reach the great hostelry known as the Profile House. You go down a number of steps and find yourself on the shore of a charming lakelet, with the pine-covered hills rising all around it, and away up above it, standing out against the sky from the mountain side, is the wonderful natural rock formation known as the Profile. It is a gigantic and most truthful side view of a human face standing out from the side of Mount Cannon, and looking across the waters of the lake to the wooded heights beyond, the wonderful freak of nature is an object of interest to all who visit this beautiful spot. Our view of the phenomenon was as nothing compared with what more fortunate travelers are favored with. The "Old Man of the Mountain," as the wonder is termed locally, had his nightcap on, and we were in too great a hurry to reach shelter before the threatening storm should break, to wait for him to take it off. The thunder was growling round us once more as we turned our backs on the lake and rode as fast as possible toward the Profile House.

You come suddenly on this noted house of entertainment among the hills. It lies in a sort of nest among the mountains, an infant plateau surrounded on all sides by towering pine-covered heights, from which there appears to be no means of egress, once you get in among them. Just as we reached the place, the threatening clouds burst almost over our heads, and we made a break up the board incline leading to the coach-house, to secure our wheels and the precious packs from what appeared a second deluge.

"You're lucky to get in," said a big stableman, "and you had better stay in, too, you can't cross a hundred yards there without being soaked through."

We were starting across to the house, but at that moment it seemed as though a cloud had burst overhead, there was a blinding flash of lightning, a deafening crash of thunder, and then a rush of water as if a continuous sheet were falling, instead of a million of separate drops. In a moment the whole road took on the semblance of a lake, and we began to understand what a storm among the hills meant.

"I guess we're booked to stay here all night," said Chester, ruefully, for we had calculated to spend the night on the other side of the mountains, in the village of Franconia.

"Oh! you're all right if you want to go on," said one of the men, "this thing won't last longer nor half an hour. Where be you going to?"

We told him we were bound for Mt. Washington, and on to Labrador, or somewhere else, and he seemed mightily surprised when he heard that we hailed from Philadelphia.

"You wait about quarter of an hour after the rain stops, and then you can ride down the mountain to Franconia without much trouble," he said.

Sure enough, the rain expended itself inside of half an hour, and as we understood the distance was inside of five miles to Franconia, and down grade, too, a treat which we had not experienced for a long time, we decided to push forward instead of putting up at the Profile for the night. A coach, the one that had come up with us, was just setting out when we started, but within five minutes we had passed it, and then commenced a-going down process which the members of the "Quartette" will probably remember as long as they live. It was one continuous descent of the mountain for about three miles. In places the rush of water had swept the roadway clear of everything but the substratum of young rocks and stones. The seething waters had carried the sandy surface down to each "thank-you-mam," and left it on its upper side, so that, when you rode up to one of these humps, the surface would appear level, but suddenly, swish! you went into about eight inches of sand and slush, then came a bump, and then a skyward elevation from the saddle, and then a useless putting on of the brake, and race, if not for life, at least for safety. It was hold on like grim death and go it, if you ever expected to get there, for to get off was merely to walk into a regular "slough of despond." If the machines could cut through the aggregations of mud and sand, and if they would but hold together over the terrible beds of exposed rocks and stones and if through it all you could keep your seat, then all right, if not all wrong.

Suddenly the clouds broke away as if by magic. We were skirting down the mountain side, and if it were not for the then uncomfortable, not to say dangerous state of affairs, I could now describe something that is but seldom seen, at any rate seldom seen by myself. I could only get a momentary glance every now and then at an enchanting picture of blue-green sky, red and amber tinted clouds, gleaming sunlight striking the tops of the hills in one quarter, and wild rolling masses of white vapor enveloping them in another. I mentally blessed that storm the one moment and mentally cursed the roadway the next, for I could not use my lips, my teeth were clenched, and my right hand was numb from holding the brake, my left little finger was in the same condition from the peculiar position I had it in holding the handle-bar, and it remained of but little use to me for the balance of the trip. Down, down, still down, it was the longest three-miles coast I had ever struck. The rest were ahead, and I had two fears, one that I should come upon one or more of them laid out for waking, or else, that I myself might be cast away on this desolate and dissolute piece of mediæval macadam, and my companions be none the wiser. Down, still down, into the dusk of the valley, with the hills getting higher and higher behind, the glorious sunset flashing redder and redder through the gaps of the hills, and that is all I knew until I almost ran smack up against a once white shirted individual whom I recognized as our usually neat and natty Laurie. He was bending over his machine. I could not stop if I wanted to, and ploughed past him through a swishing compound of mud, sand, and water. I could not even ask if he was himself or his ghost, and then I passed Chester who was also off.

"We're at the end, Laurie's broken his chain," he shouted, as I found the mud doing more for me in the way of a brake than the regular article had done or could do. "Don't get off," he continued.

I rode on for about a hundred yards, until I struck a comparatively hard spot, and then I jumped off into about two inches of red clay. Gil Wiese was some distance ahead, and after taking a momentary glance at the cloud-capped blue mountains behind us, I mounted and rode after him, half a mile to the Lafayette House, on the left of the road, where we thought it about time to call a halt.

Gilbert got in ahead, and two more sorry-looking travelers you could hardly find in a year's riding than we two as we stood on the hotel porch and looked up the road for the other half of the "Quartette." Mud! well, the backs of our white riding-shirts had changed color, there must have been a pound or so of sandy mud on them. In this element of sand was our only salvation. Had the surface of the road been clay, we would never have gotten down that grade on the machines, the wheels would have clogged inside of a few yards. As it was, however, we ran through soft spots from one-half to nearly a foot deep, the bark of which was worse than their bite, as the sand and water spurted out ahead in a kind of jet, and went off behind in the same fashion, and rolled from the hubs and spokes before having time to clog. We both had a good laugh at each other, for, to put it literally, we were sanded all over. By and by, Laurie and Chester came along, and the machines were consigned to the coach-house, and—the confession will have to be made—without cleaning, for which laziness we paid up next morning.

Talk about a place of rest for the weary, the Lafayette House was certainly such a place for us that night. Having caught some little of the rain we were naturally anxious for something to warm up the inner man and prevent danger of cold, but could not procure, before supper, anything better than champagne cider, which was about the best of its kind I ever sampled. After supper the porch was laid under requisition, and our usual programme of a smoke and a chat indulged in. Some one of the party proposed to tell stories, but the proposition fell flat. The air was damp and rather chilly, and a white mist, a legacy from the late storm, rolled down the valley.

"I don't see why we should not spin a few yarns during our travels," said Laurie. "Gil, have you not a story to tell us?"

"If you give me an hour or so to think, perhaps I may scare up something. Go ahead yourself and tell one," said Gilbert, between whiffs.

"Well, let's all agree to retail something strange or wonderful on four favorable opportunities," suggested Chester.

After some discussion, it was agreed that the plan was not such a bad one, but as no one appeared in a humor to start the ball rolling on that evening, it was voted to have the first story from Gil Wiese on the first favorable occasion, when the "Quartette" would be taking things easy.

"What will be the subject of the novel, Gil?" queried Laurie. "Recollections of the City of Washington, or Wanderings in Africa? Something lurid, you know."

"I don't know who will prove himself the biggest liar," said Gil, "but I'll do my best. Maybe I'll tell how we used to run an election in Pittsburgh."

"Mac., why don't you get up a new song for Gil, I'm tired of hearing him give us that eternal 'steady, boys, steady,' etc., that product of Washington, you know," said Laurie.

"If you help me, I will get him up one in a few minutes," the writer ventured to remark.

"Come along, then, we'll do it," said Chester, with more alacrity than had been expected of him, and forthwith Laurie and Gil were left on the porch, and the other half of the "Quartette" went into the house to hunt up some model on which to build a song for Gil. Chester hauled down a copy of Byron and broached the subject-matter of the effusion right away, from which, it is reasonable to suppose, he had been thinking of putting the job up on his companion for some time. Between the two heads and the one model the following, after much labor, was evolved.

## A SONG OF TRAVEL.

Come hither, come hither, my little foot-page,
 I'll tell you a story of love,
That was coined where the good are supposed to hang out,
 In a region that's somewhere above.

I was riding one day by the side of the way,
 With my thoughts in a heavenly jamb,
When that side-path gave out, and my thoughts in a shout
 Reached the climax of bliss in oh! ——

The side-path that looks like a maid in her teens,
 As fair as that white lily which,
If you lose your poor head, will land you, as I
 Found that side-path land me, in the ditch.

So, take warning, take warning, my little foot-page,
 And through life as you travel take care
That you keep your eye open alike when you treat
 With a side-path or maid who looks fair,
   And square,
   Or I swear
Your young heart or your pants you may tear
   Somewhere
   Or everywhere.

Whenever you want to see a new rider do his prettiest take him on a journey where a few side-paths have to be negotiated. For the matter of that, old riders very often fail to have an exalted idea of the delights of riding in a six-inch track.

# CHAPTER VIII

Lord of the hills and vales which lie below
    The great expanse of broad New Hampshire's sky,
'Tis nothing that the tempests round thee blow,
    Or that the clouds upon thy forehead lie,
'Tis nothing that the might of man has laid
    His hand upon thee, and proclaimed that thou
Art his, to cater to his will and lift
    For him thy form on high. See now
We strain to see the poise of thy proud head,
    But, in thy mute disdain of our desire
Cloudland is marshalled to repel our tread.

What a job we had after breakfast on that morning at Franconia. The chains had to be taken off all the machines, including the hickory, and the bearings of all with the exception of the hickory had to be taken off and cleaned. The wheels very nearly refused to turn at all, for between the rust and mud on them they looked more like street cleaners' paraphernalia in wet weather than like respectable bicycles.

It was after eleven o'clock before we made a start, and then having taken a few pictures, we bade adieu to the Lafayette and Franconia and made tracks for Bethlehem in New Hampshire, for dinner.

Our ultimate destination was Fabyans, the distances being Bethlehem four miles, Bethlehem Junction eight miles, Fabyans eighteen miles. The road lies up and down up and down but of course mostly up all the way. We were surprised to find the roadway on the whole fair, and going down into Bethlehem Junction, another magnificent coast repaid us for the labor of climbing. This time no storm was on hand to detract from the pleasures of rapid transit and the thank-you-mams were negotiated with comparative ease. It was getting well on into the afternoon and we were beginning to feel the calls of the inner man and nine miles lay before us to Fabyans.

" Boys," said Gilbert, " it is fair to suppose that the road ahead is by no means level; as we have decided to come back this road to Bethlehem let us train it to Fabyans."

We all looked at Gil when he thus delivered himself, but the wisdom of his proposition struck us at once. If we had one hour more all right, but even by laying the railroad under contribution we would be barely in time for supper.

" All right," said Laurie, " but I insist on riding back; we want to cover every foot of land and water at least one way by boat or bicycle."

It did not take us long to pile into the Concord & Montreal train which was just starting, and in fifteen or twenty minutes' time we found ourselves at Fabyans and under the shadow of Mount Washington. Aboard the train a better informed traveler than ourselves let us into the knowledge that if we cared less for style than comfort, the White Mountain House, about a mile below Fabyans, was a good place to put up at, so to the White Mountain House we went, and found it a hospitable stopping-place, the landlord paying us great attention and stating that he had had several cycling guests during the season already. Fabyans lies, you might say, at the foot of Mount Washington and the hotel is located almost on the railroad platform, and altogether on the direct road to the Crawford Notch.

On our reaching the noted hotel in the hills, our first thought was for a look at Mount Washington. We were disappointed in this direction, the King of the New Hampshire mountains had his crown or his cap—whichever you like to call it—pulled down over his ears, in the shape of a bank of white cloud. We wasted no time round the big hotel, or in looking for what we could not see, but turned our wheels down the road and were soon enjoying a good supper at the White Mountain House. The evening was a glorious one, the sky was not devoid of clouds, but the air was clear and the ground had benefited by the rain of the previous day, being firm, and having the dust laid, it was pleasant to both ride and walk over. Accompanied by several of the other guests at the hotel, the "Quartette" visited the pretty little waterfall that lies about three-quarters of a mile below the White Mountain House. The place is well worth visiting, the river rushing through a narrow gorge in the rocks, and running into a large dark pool below the point of curtailment. The ledges of rock are cut and worn away by the action of the fast-rushing flood into a variety of formations and the channel is almost choked up in places by the numerous logs which, cut above, have floated down and are thrown in every conceivable way on the rocks in the centre of the stream and along the sides.

On our return from the waterfall, one of our party, Mr. Myron J. Ferren, who is member for Stoneham in the Massachusetts Legislature, proposed that the "Quartette" should go up with him to Fabyans and take a look at the celebrated hostelry. We all piled into a rumbling old bus and drove the mile to the hotel. The full complement of guests were not at this immense summering resort, but, for all that, the large hall with its big open fireplace, and its wealth of Japanese fans and other light and tasty adornments was well filled with mountain sojourners, who were sitting round its wide extent reading, chatting, and otherwise amusing themselves. In the large parlor an orchestra was in full swing, with a bevy of children dancing in and out among the rich furnishings. The dining-room, a splendid hall, was evidently not yet under requisition for the large number of guests it is calculated to accommodate, and the billiard and bar rooms were also evidently waiting for the great rush of business a little later on. We were ahead of time for the big season in the mountains.

Going back in the bus with us were a few other travelers, and that mile along the railroad track, from Fabyans to the White Mountain House under the shadows of the near-by hills, resounded to the echoes of " John Brown's Body," " Annie Laurie," " McGinty," " Marching through Georgia," " The Old Oaken Bucket," and other patriotic and sentimental ditties. Coming near our stopping-place, a number of the guests turned out to see who the new arrivals were, and after we had extricated ourselves from the cavern-like depths of the lumbering conveyance, the proprietor requested that the " Quartette"—the musical one, he meant—would favor him with the "Old Oaken Bucket," of which song he was extraordinarily fond.

It was rather late for story-telling or anything of that sort when we returned from Fabyans, so not much time was spent on the porch that night, but after arranging to ride a couple of miles up the road the next morning and take a look at Mount Washington, the very comfortable beds of the White Mountain House were sought for a much-needed rest.

The sun shone brightly next morning when we bade adieu to our resting place of the night, and following the road for about two miles up after passing Fabyans and the Mount Pleasant House, we managed to see

Mount Washington with a few less clouds on it than it had boasted on the previous day. We then turned, as per the programme arranged for the rest of the trip, viz., to forego passing round to the Crawford Notch, and instead of taking in further scenes among mountains, to go back to Bethlehem, thence round through Littleton and across Vermont through a portion of the Green Mountains to Lake Champlain, and crossing the lake from Burlington, take in the much-talked-of Ausable Chasm, on the New York shore.

Mount Washington is a good-sized hill, and as such it duly impressed us, but the "Quartette" were unanimous in deciding that it would pay better to forbear making the ascent of this local lion of the hills, and instead take a more extended ride and see something more than mountains, in fact, reach the "beyond" that the New York skeptic had been doubtful of our ability to attain.

We had a glorious day for our ride back from Fabyans. Quickly the giant bulk of Mount Washington was left behind, the turns in the road and intervening hills shutting it out from view every now and then. Then Twin Mountain came into view to the left, while also to the left and away in the valley below us leaped and tumbled the little stream, the music of whose waters would every now and then creep up to us. The Twin Mountain House, sitting on a high knoll facing the eminence from which it derives its name, was soon left behind and we drew near to Bethlehem Junction. From this place on to Bethlehem we had to climb the steep grade of several miles, which had been such a welcome coast coming the other way. Bethlehem reached, however, we had our reward, for, running down on the road to Littleton, we had the finest coast up to that time struck on the trip. The grade was not very steep, and the road surface was excellent. The machines fairly flew, and given much of this kind of riding we had no doubt as to our ability to reach St. Johnsbury, where we purposed stopping for the night. We had wished very much to reach Burlington on Lake Champlain by Saturday night, as by that time we would have been exactly two weeks on the road, but on looking up data and finding that but little could be done in Burlington on Sunday, no boats crossing the lake on that day, it was resolved to take things easy through the beautiful green country ahead of us, stop at St. Johnsbury Friday night, the 17th, Montpelier Saturday night, and Burlington Sunday. It was just as well we decided on this programme, for the road between Montpelier and Burlington, at least the valley portion of it lying to the right of the noted Camel's Hump Mountain, was terribly sandy and proved most exasperating for bicycle riding.

Well, to go back to that grand coast after leaving Bethlehem. We were still in New Hampshire, with the pretty summering place of Littleton for our first stopping-place. It was almost dinner time when the "Quartette" pulled up at the Littleton House, and on dismounting were almost immediately joined by a local wheelman, Mr. F. B. Sawyer, mounted on an "Eagle" bicycle, who turned out to be the local L. A. W. Consul. He was extremely kind and accompanied us about a mile outside the town on our leaving it after dinner.

He informed us that some Philadelphia riders had passed up to the mountains about a month previous, and had stopped at Littleton. We looked the matter up and found that they were Messrs. Mitchell, Elliott, and Nelms of our own club, who had been on an outing through the Berkshire hills and had extended their trip through Montpelier and Littleton to the district we had just left behind.

At the Littleton House Gil Wiese was in his element. A couple of those strolling players who are constantly on the move throughout the summer resorts of the hill country, happened to be at the hotel and started playing in the general room. Gil kept them there during the hour of rest after the mid-day meal, and whether it was the peculiar manner in which the dark-skinned sons of Italy handled the harp and the fiddle, or whether it was that the three different kinds of pie which our companion had sampled proved too much for his equanimity, it is a fact that our musical member became of the color generally characteristic of bilious individuals at sea, and for the space of half an hour at the hotel, and two hours on the road afterward, he was not in exactly the condition that robust and healthy wheelmen like to be. Nevertheless the "Quartette" rode into St. Johnsbury that evening sound in mind and body. This little incident is mentioned as being the only case of an approach to illness among the members of the "Quartette" during the entire trip, and possibly the extreme heat of the day had something to do with creating this single break in the monotony of good health.

We had struck some good riding running into Littleton, but it was on leaving this noted summer resort that we dropped upon some of the most enjoyable ups and downs of what to that date had been a most up and down excursion.

Our route from Littleton lay through Waterford, and to reach the Vermont side we had to cross the Connecticut River, which is at this point a wide stream. A bridge is in course of construction now on the site of an old structure, and pending its completion travelers are ferried across on a large float. Not knowing the topography of the place, we passed this ferrying point about a quarter of a mile before finding out our mistake. Some farm hands on the far side of the river, noting us going down the road, and guessing our desired route, shouted to us and motioned us back, and without much difficulty we found the semi-byway leading down to the ford. The float, which carries wagons as well as pedestrians, makes the cross-stream trip by means of a rope swung across the stream on which are rings and pulleys, and the novel stage is attached to these by other ropes, and is part poled across by the man in charge, and partly carried across by the action of the current. Laurie took a picture of the waterman and his craft, but this tribute did not prevent the sunburned knight of the pole and pulley from levying on us the customary tribute of a few cents for the short voyage. It was from this point that we struck some of the enjoyable riding referred to above. Splendid coasts under arches of grand trees, and oftentimes along the sides of hills whose green sides, together with the green fields of the valleys and also of the opposite ranges of hills, give ample evidence of the reason why Vermont should hold the name it does, and why it should have the Green Mountains within its borders.

The only time when the "Quartette" so far forgot its dignity and its rules of travel as to indulge in road-racing was on the dusty and, at times, rutty macadam road running into St. Johnsbury. A supposed denizen of that neighborhood with his supposed best girl in the buggy with him passed the party, making no bones about taking the best portion of the road to himself and his horse and his accompanying load of sweet seventeen more or less, and he evidently thought that by whipping up his Vermont trotter he could leave the "Quartette" of pedal-pushers far in the rear. He did leave us for a season, but after about a mile and a half, after missing him, coming round a bend in the road, we drew up with him again. Owing to the hilly configuration of the country it is impossible, especially as the "Quartette" is a very modest one, especially in the matter of its own achievements, to tell our readers exactly why it was we caught up. Whether it was because we were fast riders or because the lord of the buggy had been taking advantage of the romantic loneliness and loveliness of the surroundings to whisper lovely things to the second occupant of the vehicle. Whatever the reason, we came right up on the handler of the whip and ribbons and passed him. Evidently our return of his compliment to us did not please him or the lady, for on the first opportunity the whip was brought into requisition and the Vermont trotter responded to a spanking by passing us the second time. "Well!" said the "Quartette," "we will let him alone for a while until a good chance occurs, and then we will see what his trotter is made of." Accordingly, a respectful distance was maintained in the rear of the Green Mountain Maud S. until the rise of the ground commenced going up to St. Johnsbury, when, on the up-grade, the "Quartette" drew close up behind and watched for what was to come. At the top of the grade and in sight of the town the driver again whipped up his nag, but this time the pedal-pushers kept close up behind, though the dust was something fearful. Next thing the trotting genius knew was that one-half of the "Quartette" were by and speeding along the level into St. Johnsbury. Then there was a vigorous plying of the whip, and a quarter-mile dash followed in which the horse and buggy come off second best, clean up to the big hill in the middle of the town to the no small edification of a number of citizens, who evidently enjoyed the spectacle and sympathized with the bicyclers.

The "Quartette" lodged that night at the Avenue House.

St. Johnsbury did not possess sufficient attractions to tempt us on an investigating tour after supper. Recourse to the hotel porch was there-fore in order, and while enjoying the regular rest after the day's ride, with a quiet smoke for one-half of the "Quartette," Chester proposed that "Gil" should tell the story which he had promised. Our fourth portion acquiesced, and with the prefatory statement that he was no story-teller and that his tale would be brief, started as follows:

### "A PITTSBURGH ELECTION.

"You may give Pittsburgh credit for being a smoky city, but there are many bright things there, as well as many dark things, some bright men and some bright women."

"Really, now; well, I'm surprised," drawled the dry and caustic Laurie. Laurie could be caustic, we found that out, although his tempera-ment is generally the reverse.

"Facts are facts, and surprise don't make or unmake them," was the rejoinder blown back by the story-teller in a cloud of cigarette odor, which, by the way, Laurie detested.

"Well, as I was saying," pursued Gilbert, "Pittsburgh is a very good city—good for business, good to live in, good for politics, as Chris Magee makes pretty plain to your Philadelphia head-cook, Matthew Stanley Quay, who, it would seem, has cooked his goose a little too brown of late, and who may have consequently less gravy in the future than he has had in the past. There are other politicians in Pittsburgh and Allegheny City, however, besides Chris Magee, and some of them have long heads, too, as you shall see when I tell you how John Michael Carroll put his man in from a ward very near to ours in the big city on the Allegheny.

"John-Michael is a pretty strong name combination, if I recollect my religious education right, to say nothing of the Carroll part of it. But plain 'Mike' or 'Mickey' was the appellation which this great power in his division was known by, and it must have been in his case the essence of Judea and Hibernia boiled down into one strong condiment that made the name of 'Mickey' a tower of strength in the —— division of the —— Ward.

" But to get down to business. There was a hot time one fall in Allegheny City and Pittsburgh, and while general issues did not run high, the local-issue pot was just boiling over, because there was some glory and considerable money depending on the result of what was a close fight.

" Of course, 'Mickey' was in it, and every one knew that the matter of a very few votes, no matter how they came, or where they came from, would swing things either way. Well, though Mickey lives in a big house now, and has an odd dollar to spend on the boys now and then, at that time he was in as tight a financial place as his party was in a tight political one, and the worst of it was that he had nothing but his name to raise the wherewithal on. His name was all right, it was a thing to swear by in the district, but scarcely good enough security to loan money on, especially in troublesome times such as then existed for himself and his friends. One night some of us were at the club, where it was customary for us to gather to chat over local matters and sing a few songs, for some of us were struck in the musical way, and who should walk in but 'Mickey.'

" 'Hello, " Mickey the Mighty," how goes things?' sang out Will. Will is enough to designate one of the jolliest fellows in our crowd in those days. 'How goes it, Mickey ? Will Develin go through all right ?'

" 'That's more than I can tell, or you either, the way things is goin', now,' replied the new arrival, and then he continued, 'I want to see a couple of you fellows, Will and Jake there, and you, Johnson.'

" We went over to a corner of the room with the light of the —— ward, and his first words were :

" ' Boys, I want just $100.'

" 'You come the wrong place to get it, old man. Look at that,' said Will, and at the same time he pulled out a brown morocco case he always carried, and laid a ten-dollar bill, a five, and three ones on the table. 'We're all poor here; but what do you want it for, bail ?'

" ' There is not much use in saying what I want it for, but I tell you what the ward wants, it wants to win in to-morrow's fight just 89½ votes, that's what the ward wants—no matter what I want.'

" 'Eighty-nine and a half votes,' we all repeated, with a heavy stress laid on the *half*. ' What on earth do you mean, Mike, by a half vote ?'

" 'Never mind what I mean, it's just as I say. We want 89½ votes to win the grandest fight we've had here for ages. Now, who's the man to put up $100, if I go on record to win the fight ?'

" ' Won't $89½ do, Mickey ?' queried Jake, laughingly, 'anyhow, where does that half vote come in ?'

" John Michael looked very wise as he said :

" 'That's my business; you can bet I've got down to close figuring when I get into half votes.'

" ' That's the funniest thing I ever heard of,' said Will, while Johnson looked at Michael as though he thought he had been out too long with the boys. 'Look here, now, can I have that hundred, I'll give security,' said Mike.

" ' Never mind the security, tell us about the mutilated vote ; the explanation may be worth fifty,' said Johnson.

" ' Well it's a matter of logic and common sense, is that half vote,' said the would-be borrower. ' I'll take fifty for telling who the half vote is, and, as I said before, I'll give security for the other fifty, if you'll only put the money up.'

" ' We're good for fifty anyhow, and maybe for more, on good security. Go ahead and relieve our curiosity, Mickey,' said Johnson.

" 'And yez are good for the money, are yez ?' put in the cautious Michael, relapsing for the moment into his old-time vernacular.

" ' Of course we are, go on,' was the chorus from the crowd around him.

" A broad grin overspread Michael's face.

" ' Faith then,' he said, ' it's just this way. You know Fritz Guigenheimer, boys, good Fritz, the best Dutch Republican I ever run against. Well, you know, he got married six months ago, to as pretty a little woman as ever walked in Pittsburgh, but faith the beauty's all spoiled, all on account of her bein' one of them temperance crowd, over the hill there, she played the mischief with Fritz up to a week ago ; but he's feelin' better now, I guess, seein' he's half booked to vote the Democratic ticket to-morrow.'

" ' Yes, we all know Fritz, but about the half vote, the half vote, that's what we want,' we all cried.

" ' Well, an' isn't that what I'm comin' to, haven't yez any patience while I'm talkin' about the ladies, and wan of the best of them at that. But, anyhow, here's the whole story of the half, and I hope ye'll all be satisfied. Fritz and his wife is wan, isn't they now,' and Michael again dropped into the vernacular. ' Now, I've got the wife, and bein' as the two is wan, and I have wan, and the wan or the two, whichever yez like, has a vote, and I have the half of the one, aint I got half of a vote, aint I now ?'

" The earnestness with which this unique story was given threw us all into convulsions of laughter.

" ' Mickey, you can reason like a Harvard professor,' said Will, be-tween the peals of laughter.

" ' Oh ! but wait, I haven't told yez all, wait till I tell yez the strategy, raal Ginral Grant strategy, I employed to get the half. Ye see Fritz got let off to go down to that nest of pirates, at the Jim Blaine Club, No. 3, where the other side works from, just for an hour once a week. Well, he filled his wife up full with the notion that the Republicans were to fight against rum, in all shape and form, and I knew it, and I says to meself, Fritz, me boy, if I can fill you up full of the best whisky that ever came out of ould Ireland, your vote's mine. And I did it. It wasn't right by the little woman, boys, was it ? but what business had the fellow goin' and makin' out to her that the Republicans in the ward were all saints and the rest of us sinners. Yes, that woman believes that if the Republicans win, the whole country, law, order, and everything else will " bust " sure. She's bound Fritz will vote the Democratic ticket this time, and don't you forget it.'

" ' Mickey, you ought to be ashamed of yourself, breaking up the domestic felicity of a worthy man,' said Will, with mock solemnity.

" ' Domestic felicity ! what's domestic felicity where a vote's consarned, and haven't I me own domestic felicity, as you call it, to look out for, but yez see, here's just how we managed it.

" ' I had Mary Casey tip the wink to the old woman that it was goin' the rounds that her husband went home from the club along with half a dozen of the boys with more happiness in his heart than his sweet little new wife could put there. Of course there was a devil of a row among the women over it, and Mrs. Fritz indignantly denied the allegation, and wanted to know who dared spread such reports about her husband. Well, two nights after there was a big deal to be fixed, and a certain party fixed Fritz, so he should have just enough as was good for him, and he walked home feelin' as though he was runnin' the whole division. I don't know what happened that night, but Fritz went home straight after the next meetin'. The next time, however, when the big caucus was over, some of the boys got together, and a couple of friends of mine got in with the crowd and engineered things so nice that happiness was no name for their frame of mind, and though Fritz walked home as straight as wan of the bulrushes that didn't bend over to look at little Moses in his cradle, still he had a dozen cigars in his pocket and a pretty little light in his eye, in case he didn't have a match in the other pocket. Well, that fixed it, with what Mary Casey said about we Democrats being dead set ag'in liquor; and Mrs. Fritz Guigenheimer swore in her own manner, up and down that Fritz shouldn't go any more to the " Jim Blaine, No. 3," and that he should vote the Democratic ticket, if she had to go to the polls and see him do it. There, now, what do you think of that for a half vote anyhow ? Where's that hundred ?'

"'Mickey, you don't deserve anything, you rascal; indeed you don't,' said Will, who had enjoyed the recital, as he did any piece of clever fun, but where's the security for the other fifty? you're a great worker, and you deserve help, but you're an awful schemer.'

"'If I get that hundred, I'll get the best part of the 89½ votes we want. Come along, you fellows, and I'll show you the security.'

" Curiosity led us to follow Michael round a few blocks and up to the hill lying some distance from our meeting place.

" ' There, do you see that house sitting right up there near the top of that hill, there's me security.' ' But you don't own it, Mickey. You're going crazy, I think,' said Johnson, eying him suspiciously. 'Oh! but I will, though, if this thing goes the way we want it. You just let me get them 89½ votes, and that house is mine, and $100 won't be a drop in the bucket for me to fix up. Come now, boys, you won't see me left for a mean little hundred.'

" The upshot of the thing was that Michael got his $100 on the security of his well-known ability as a worker, backed by his prospective ownership of real estate.

" The night after the election, he turned up where we were all gathered at the club-house and handed a large envelope to Will, saying, as he swelled his big chest out,

"'There you are, gentlemen, there's your $100, and many thanks. On the strength of the win yesterday I borrowed a loan, I did, and first thing pay back me just dues.'

"' But how did you get your 89½ votes. Mickey, tell us that,' said Will.

"' Ninety votes if you please, and 90 to the back of them, 90, gentlemen, because the half wan turned into a whole wan, whin Mrs. Fritz Guigenheimer walked up to the polls and kept an eye on the little man Fritz. But yez want to know about the votes, well here's how 47 of 'em came anyhow—are yez all true blue?'

" There were seven of us, and we were all, as Michael said, ' true blue.'

"' Do you know, boys, what I did with that little $100. I just laid in a big stock of victuals and drink, with the balance of quantity slightly on the side of the latter article, and with the cash left over I went down to Isaac Isaacs and says I,

"'"Isaac, you're a good Democrat"—I knew he wasn't, you know—

"now don't you think you ought to get the contract for the suits for those Italian pavers who are going to be fixed up by our friend —— to work across the river for one year?"

"'"Sure," says Isaac, "sure, I can make those garmints that I have in stock sell at almost nothing prices for those men."

"'"Well," I says, "if there's enough votes the right way to-morrow you gets the job, and lots more. Have you any relations, Isaac, over-age ones. I mean citizens, you know?"

"'"Oh! yesh, yesh, lotsh, lotsh, hundreds I have—"

"'"There, that will do, Isaac; as an earnest of what I say, I will buy a couple of dozen of these old hats, a dozen and a half of those second-hand coats, and that bundle of odd sizes of pants there. How much?" The descendant of Oriental traders charged just twice as much as the things were worth, but you bet the good cause did not suffer.

"'"Isaac," I said, "I want these things for my wife, she is dead struck on the Indians out West, poor souls, and some of them haven't a rag to their backs."

"'"Ze poor creatures," said good Isaac, with a grin, "don't ze dear savage red man want some of deze neckties, dey is sheep, vera sheep."

"'"No, thank you, Isaac, no, thank you," I said, "my wife can't expect me to buy her protegees—I said protegees—gold watches and neckties in addition to the regular articles of civilized wear."

"'"Vera well, I will tink veramuch to-night and to-morrow about ze other matter."

"'"Do, Isaac, do," I said, "you will find it to your advantage to do so, my friend," and then I walked home.

"'Now, boys, it's a hard thing to say, but it's a fact, can't help it being one, that more happy men went to the polls from our division yesterday, before the result was known, than went to sleep after it.'

"'Mickey, you're a great rascal,' said Johnson.

"Michael paid no attention to the remark, but continued: 'You should have seen old man Dunkleberger, after voting. Some of the boys had him round to the house. He was very foolish, when he got there, to mistake champagne for cider, and after that to mistake one of Isaac's old hats and coats for brand-new goods straight from Zusky's and swap his own off for them, and then, most strange to say, he forgot he had voted and would insist on going to the polls again, and, stranger still, he made the same mistake later in the day when, in company with Doc. Adams, he went to get shaved, and the barber, mistaking orders, trimmed his whiskers goatee fashion, and his own wife did not want to let him in the house. The old man got his back up, and blest if he didn't have Doc. take him round to vote again, as he fancied he was a fellow named Jigger or Jagger who had moved away from the division two years ago.

"'It was a great stroke of policy, it was more, it was strategy, downright strategy, boys,' and as he thus delivered himself Michael lay back in his chair and looked every inch a 'Ginral Grant,' as he said himself. Then a twinkle came in his eye as he said:

"'I was goin' to forget the best thing of the whole business. That confounded old Isaac came round to the house this morning, and what do you suppose he wanted?'

"'Suppose he wanted to tell you he had voted the right way and wanted the contract,' said Johnson.

"'The divil a bit, he knew very well I knew how he voted. Do you know what the old sinner came after? Why, he wanted to turn purchaser himself. "My dear Mr. Carroll," says he, "an' does ze Mrs. Carroll still want those goods for ze poor Indians. I vill buy zum back if freights is too high just now." Do you know I liked the grasping old son of Abraham and I let him have the whole lot, minus three hats and two coats for 25 cents. And that's how we did the business, boys. Pretty neat, wasn't it, and there's your money back and many thanks for the accommodation.'

"Michael put on his hat, a new silk one, by the way, and went out, while we discussed what had been to us an incident of peculiar interest. It is a fact that John Michael Carroll very shortly afterward acquired by purchase the property he pointed out to us on the hill the night before that election, and there is not a man now among his friends in Pittsburgh who would question his ability to repay the loan of a hundred dollars a hundred times over.

"There, now, the ' Quartette ' has had my story for all it is worth. It's time to turn in," and forthwith the four travelers retired to dream of high hills and honest politics.

# CHAPTER IX.

## ACROSS VERMONT.

Green are the hills and the valleys
And green is each mountain chain,
That, stretching across the fair Vermont
Sweeps down to the broad Champlain ;
There Mansfield rears on high its head
Where the clouds in jealous rest
Are holding council in billowy folds
Flung over its lordly crest,
And the Camel's Hump with curving line
Cut clear where the cloudland ends,
And marking against the blue a blot
That back to the traveler sends
Sweet thoughts of the hills and vales that lie
In New Hampshire and in Maine ;
Now left behind that with flowing sail
He may sweep o'er broad Champlain.

At St. Johnsbury the symmetry of the "Quartette" suffered a sad blow. Our hard-riding, good natured Chester had to leave us. We had been two weeks on the road, and it was imperative that he should be home by the following Monday, so, on the morning of Saturday, the three-fourths of the "Quartette" took a sorrowful farewell of the departing one-fourth, and sent one of the best of traveling companions booming down the Passumpsic Railroad, on his way to New York. We were extremely sorry to lose our Chester, and thought that in parting company at St. Johnsbury we had lost the story, which, as a member of the roving band, he had promised to contribute for the edification of the whole. It was an agreeable surprise, therefore, when, jumping on the train, he handed a roll of paper to Laurie, saying: "There, boys, is my contribution to the narrative bargain. You will forgive me for its dryness. Good-bye, and good luck for the rest of the trip."

We ran out of St. Johnsbury down a short grade, passing the noted Fairbanks Scales Works on our left, and crossing a small wooden bridge, bore still to the left, and climbed a good-sized hill which took us away above the level of the town. The road was a very fair one. Our route, according to directions, lay through Danville and Marshfield, a distance of some 35 miles to Montpelier, the capital of the State. There was plenty of time to make the run, as the programme was to stop at Montpelier that night, and go on the next day to Burlington on the lake. It would have been a pity, or, as Laurie said, "a downright sin," to make time in such a lovely country. The roads were superb as far as surface went, and in the way of scenery in the rural picturesque line the country was all that could be desired. "A second Ireland," averred Laurie, and he was right. Down long slopes with feet on the foot-rests, dispensing altogether with the labor of pedaling; up long grades, walking where there was any disposition to feel tired ; skirting along the sides of hills the party went, at a rate of speed calculated to give a chance for a thorough enjoyment of the eminently rural region through which our route lay. The road between Danville and St. Johnsbury is very generally traveled, and there were in parts some few ruts to try our patience, but otherwise there was nothing to complain of about the highway. When near Marshfield, a two-horse wagon with five men in it, returning from some race-meeting, was encountered. The men were pretty good fellows, and pulled up to ask about the machines, the wooden one especially attracting their attention. They waited for us to start in order to see if we could mount the hill which they had just come down, which feat—a great one to them—we successfully accomplished.

Just outside of Marshfield, and from the high ground overlooking the place, we obtained a very good view across a picturesque country, and just at this point there is a half-natural, half-artificial waterfall, on the Onions River, or as it is called now, the Winooski River, which latter is doubtless its original title, again bestowed on what lower down is a beautiful stream. The cameras had again to be unstrapped at this point, and about an hour was spent clambering up and down the waterfall, catching beauties of rock and water under different auspices. There was a wealth of raspberries round this neighborhood, and a few minutes' industrious picking resulted in quite a luxurious feed off of the red, ripe fruit. Some sand was struck in this neighborhood, but not very much. I neglected to mention that, getting hungry, we did not wait for dinner until we got to Marshfield, but made a meal at a farmer's house by the roadside, near Joe's Pond, a little lakelet, so named after some old Indian by the name of Joe, who has thus left a most prosaic title for a very pretty little sheet of water. The main portion of our meal, as far as quantity went, seemed to be maple sugar, for a large basket of the toothsome commodity was broken open in our honor. After the meal, the trees from which the sugar was derived were shown to us.

On leaving Marshfield, it became evident that rain was in store for us, and the pace was quickened in order to get into Montpelier ahead of the threatened dampness, which, most fortunately, was a thing that up to that time had not troubled us much on the trip. Also, at Montpelier we expected to find the grip, which had been traveling all round the country from Boston and North Conway, and which contained films for the cameras, and articles of clothing which the writer was most anxious to have, as common string was scarcely the thing with which to darn stockings, and a gray shirt that had once been white was not the most pleasant or presentable garment to appear in in public. About two miles outside of Montpelier the rain came down pretty lively, and there was a medium mild scorch into town. The big clock was striking six when the writer pulled up at the express office, just as the clerk was locking up to go out for supper. In answer to the demand for a grip came the answer that there was no grip there, and a mixture of anger and disappointment was carried with the now broken "Quartette" to the post-office, and thence to the Montpelier House.

Gil got quite a grist of letters at this point. He had calculated on getting to Montpelier two days before we did, and had his generally voluminous correspondence directed to the capital of Vermont, so as to be absolutely sure of getting it. The mail was all right, but the writer's grip was all wrong, and a telegram was at once forwarded to North Conway to see what was the matter, with orders to forward the much-needed paraphernalia to Burlington.

The rain came down heavily all the evening, much after the fashion that it did at Plymouth, Mass., and there was nothing to do but stay in-doors after supper, or sit on some dry corner of the porch. Very little information could be gained as to the best road for bicycles to Burlington, through

Waterbury, however, being the way that seemed to have the most favor, and thence by way of Richmond, leaving Essex Junction severely alone, and bearing to the left through Williston and Burlington. This was the longest way, but it was said to be the best. After we had sampled it we wondered what the worst could be like.

There being nothing but rain outside the house, and not very much to be done inside but talk and smoke, it was a very natural thing to call up the story-telling project, and as our departed Chester's contribution was all cut and dry in Laurie's pocket, that worthy was directed to bring the same out and read it, and being as curious as the rest of us to see what the younger scion of his house had to say, it needed no coaxing to bring forth the pencil-written tale of Chester, which, read by his brother, ran as follows:

### " MY SUMMER GIRL.

"' Lightly blew the breezes over Lake George. Bright shone the sun over the royal sheet of water where I spent so many happy hours, and the beauties of which the balance of the " Quartette " will, no doubt, be enjoying when I am once more in harness digging and delving amidst the wilderness of brick and stone and mortar known as Philadelphia.

"' I was on the lake in a light skiff—I am on it again in imagination. I see the same ripples skimming over the placid water, I see the same beautiful blue sky above me, and the same grand hills closing in around me and jealously guarding myself and my treasure, and I hear again the soft voice, soft when whispering and soft when raised in laughter, that was then more than the world to me, and that now is a remembrance as pleasant in separation as it was then a beatific vision of loveliness in palpable and tangible presence.

"' I hear you fellows saying :

"' " Come, now, what are you giving us," and I say in reply nothing but what is fact, nothing but what fortunately or unfortunately for myself was an incident in a life which has up to the present been singularly devoid of accident, and, with one or two exceptions, absolutely free from the sentimental entanglements which are considered inseparable from youth and young blood.' "

" Hold on there, Laurie," said Gil, " you're making that up. I won't believe Chester wrote any such stuff as that. Let me look."

" Honest, Gil, it's all here. I don't know what the fellow is driving at myself," said Laurie, whose eyes, as he read, had been growing to dimensions that resembled those of the conventional saucer. " What's he going to write about, anyhow ?" continued Laurie, running his eyes down the manuscript.

" Never mind; if you're not humbugging go ahead and read," said Gil, settling himself down in the cane-bottomed chair he occupied, and lighting a cigarette with an air of resignation.

Laurie scratched his chin in a vain search for the whiskers he was wont to pull under exciting or puzzling contingencies, and proceeded as follows:

"' It was a dream, a glorious dream. A vision of what life might be, and, no doubt, what life was intended to be before the development of what the world is pleased to call science invaded the realm of nature and sentiment, and commenced to govern the actions of men and things with a line of wire, or a puff of second-hand water. It was a dream, I repeat, that summer by the bright waters of the royal lake—a dream to be caught and held in the golden frame of memory as long as the life lasts that was then brightened by its existence.' "

" God bless him ; he talks like a book," said Gil, and that was all Gil said during the remainder of the reading of Chester's story. Laurie proceeded :

" ' I met Myra—never mind her second name—the summer a few years ago, that I was stopping at Caldwell, on Lake George. It was one of those acquaintanceships which, formed at such summering-places, rarely last longer than the circumstances or relationships which are answerable for their existence. But if any one had told me, if any one had ventured to even hint to me that Myra and myself should ever think less of each other than we did during that happy summer, I should have thought such statement ample cause for the demanding of satisfaction in some shape or other at the hands of the embodiment of temerity making it.

" ' Yes, Myra was a " daisy." She was a " corker," and no mistake about it.

" ' There are times and seasons when the heart, feeling what the lips fail to convey through the medium of words, has recourse to other means of imparting a knowledge of emotions that, springing from the inmost recesses of the soul, are on this earth, to my mind, a foretaste of what we may expect to be the joys of that future life which we are taught to look for. It was such a time with me, that summer which I refer to, when, with Myra as well as with myself, the heart, too full for utterance by means of the lips, spoke with more than a passionate eloquence through the eyes, through every feature, and through every action, in a way which seemed to show that heaven, for at least two souls, had been anticipated on earth.

" ' We met by chance, as it were, at the summering house of a mutual friend. She drove there in her pony cart—I had ridden there on my bicycle. A week later one wheel was off the pony cart and my bicycle had gone to the blacksmith's, and she and I—I, at any rate—were floating in a dream of ecstasy on that glorious dream of water known as Lake George.

" ' Truly she was my Myra, she was my first, my one and only love. One week had done the business. It seemed to me we were all in all to each other.

" ' Forgive me if I again say she, my Myra, was a " daisy," a regular " jim dandy," a " corker " from away back. In a week's time I was her slavey forever. But to return to that one day the memory of which, like the echo of some sweet and lost song, haunts me still, and causes me at moments of retrospective leisure or of undisturbed meditation to question the eternal fitness of things as far as their relationship goes toward the beating of two hearts as one. To return, I say. The sun shone slanting through the hills and across the waters of the lake—waters stirred only into the tiniest ripples by but a baby breeze, ripples beside which the ones awakened to life by the dipping of my oars appeared as great waves. Over the sleeping woods, over the silver bosom of the lake, dwelt a great quiet, an all-pervading restfulness that offered, could my inmost self have been as open to an observer as was the face of nature round me, a marked and wonderful contrast to the tumult going on within me. She was with me, reclining in the stern of the skiff, both fair hands trailing in the softly-lapping ripples along the sides of the frail craft, her glorious blue eyes gazing into mine with a wealth of meaning that to me conveyed but one thought, nay, one belief, and that was the belief that she loved me. And I ran the boat in where the great elbow of a hill threw its dark shadow over the little cove nestling at its base, and I sat and gazed into those eyes and listened to those rosy lips laugh words of music that were sweeter to me then than a first mortgage on a seraph's song in Paradise. And the shadows lengthened over the miles of darkening water, and a silver streak crept across the wavering ripples from where the moon was rising between the hills, and I said : " Myra, may I tell you something ?"

" ' " Certainly, what is it ?"

" ' " Myra, you can make me happy."

" ' "I thought I had done so, I thought you looked real happy and I think so still."

" ' " But, Myra, you know what I mean. Myra, I love you ; will you take me for what I am, will you make me the happiest fellow on earth ?"

" ' " What's that ! make you what you imagine would be the happiest fellow on earth and myself the most miserable girl in America ?"

" ' " What do you take me for, Myra ?"

" ' " Why for a decidedly big fool for a boy of your age. Take your oars up, sir, and row me ashore."

" ' And I rowed her ashore, and I thought then as I say now, that she was the corkingest, finest girl that ever hooked a fellow into trouble or made him pull out of it.' "

Laurie laid down the paper and looked round at us. " That's all of it," he said.

" Well, if I had not traveled for two weeks with Chester, I'd say he was telling rather too good a story, but I do believe there is something in it," said Gil, and then the " Quartette " turned in, to dream dreams and see visions of what lay ahead, where Lakes Champlain and George barred the land passage to the West.

Sundry were the maledictions felt, if not poured forth in words the next morning by the writer on the heads of all express companies, their clerks, etc., who handle grips and such like baggage through the mountain world of New Hampshire.

" Positively, I will not wear this thing any longer," I said, throwing my sateen riding shirt, begrimed and stained with sand and mud from our late experiences, into a corner of the room.

" You know the old saying," said Gil, who was my room-mate. "Don't throw out the dirty water, etc."

" I don't care," I said, "I will get that grip at Burlington, and we will reach Burlington to-night."

" It's going to be hot to-day, and you don't want to ride in your coat," said Gil, " put the thing on, who cares for you or your white shirt up here ?"

I sat on the side of the bed and looked ruefully at the bright sunlight creeping in through the curtains ; suddenly a thought struck me, one of those " happy thoughts," F. C. Burnand thoughts, such as the noted humorist used to decorate the pages of *Punch* with.

" Gil," I said, " do you think they would ever know the difference ?"

" What difference, and who do you mean ?"

" Why, the difference between that," and I pointed to the bundle of soiled linen in the corner, and the comparatively spotless garment of night wear I was about to roll off and put in the bundle.

" Capital," said Gil, " but it's too fancy about the collar, and it's too long."

" The collar may be fancy, Gil, but I've seen fancier."

" Not on a bicycle rider, or in broad daylight ; but wear it, man, what's the odds ?"

" I think I will ; as for the length, Gil, the saddle felt awful hard, yesterday."

"Oh! the length is all right, it's the collar they might get on to; who knows about the length unless you wear the thing Chinese fashion? But you can fix the objection at one end anyhow; why not cut it off?"

"That's the ticket; but we have not Chester any more, and he has the scissors."

"No; Laurie has Chester's work-basket or work-bag, needles, thread, shears, and all the rest of it, and I want to mend this stocking," said Gil.

In a few minutes' time the bundle of linen in the corner was increased, and a most comfortable night-robe suffered a mutilation from which it never recovered, and in fifteen minutes' time, with coat buttoned tightly up at the throat, I once more felt like the proverbial Richard—a poor one, no doubt, but happy—and we three, instead of four, sampled breakfast.

Under a bright sun and over a muddy road, the journey was again resumed through Montpelier and out into the open country toward Waterbury. Montpelier is a pretty town, with plenty of foliage surrounding and bending over the many handsome houses setting well back from the wide main street that leads in and out of Vermont's capital.

Agreeable to the riding code of the Pennsylvania Bicycle Club we wore our coats while passing through the town, but when well outside consigned them to their regular place on the handle-bar, and then the laugh for a few miles turned on the wearer of what Laurie wanted a picture of very badly, but we reminded him that, in the absence of the grip and the new films, we wanted all that was in the cameras for the beauties of nature and not of art.

At the start the roads were slightly heavy, but as the day wore on the effects of the last night's rain wore off, and a fair road-surface carried us into Waterbury in time for dinner at noon. Beyond the great watch factory and some handsome residences, there is nothing in Waterbury to need special notice, and at 2 o'clock the road was again taken, with directions to follow the windings of the beautiful Winooski River through the hills to Bolton, Richmond, and Burlington. The road was said to be good by parties whom we inquired of, but we found it only passable, and in some places simply unridable, where it ran between two ranges of hills, between which wound the river over a sandy bottom. Near Bolton we ran across one of the most beautiful little waterfalls which we had struck. Leaving the machines on the roadside, and guided by a farmer's lad, whom the present of a cigar tempted off the fence on which he was sitting, we descended a steep declivity through a bunch of woods to where the now noisy Winooski broke through a narrow gorge of the hills. There is one main fall, and then the river cuts through a young cañon, the rocks being worn away and carved into many curious shapes. In several instances we noted circular holes, cut down or up, as the case might be, through immense rocks, much in the same fashion as if they had been drilled artificially. Away up above us towered a mass of rock, which, cutting clear against the beautiful blue sky, seemed as though it might be the ever-watchful and grim guardian of this most beautiful spot.

From our guide we learned that a little lower down the stream there was a large cave, which was often visited by tourists. We had spent an hour at the falls, and did not feel like going further down and crossing the stream to see the cave, so proceeded on toward Richmond. I neglected to mention that, in the first half of the day, we had gone some four miles out of our way by turning up Mud or Mad river. Whichever name it is we considered ourselves and our wheels mud when we found out our mistake, and had to retrace our course.

The little hamlet of Bolton lies near the end of a long valley, or rather at a point where the valley narrows in. All through this valley several miles in length, runs the railroad and the river, as well as the road, if you can call it a road. Owing to the predominance of sand, a great deal of walking had to be done, and many were the blessings breathed when, beyond Bolton, higher ground with a harder surface was struck. By the time the little town of Richmond appeared ahead, we were somewhat hungry, having been delayed by a couple of showers, which, as a legacy from the storm of the previous night, came up to spoil what was otherwise a perfect day.

Supper at Richmond, and then on for Burlington. The proprietor of the hotel advised us to to remain over-night at Richmond, but we wanted to reach Burlington that evening, so as to be on hand for the boat next morning at eight o'clock, for our visit to the Ausable Chasm on the other side of Lake Champlain. It was a 45-mile ride from Montpelier to Burlington by the way we had come, and from Richmond in by way of Williston the distance was about 15 miles. A good portion of this had to be ridden in the dark, and did we not wish for the moon to rise sooner than we knew it would ! The first few miles saw good roads, then the travel became poor, and just as we were getting somewhat cross over the possibility of another Shepard Hill ride, on turning round by way of Williston, the highway became a little more ridable, and for several miles without light of lamps or moon, pot luck in the way of immunity from falls was taken along a very fair horsetrack, running in the middle of a very hard surfaced road.

When within about five or six miles of Burlington, however, the good road left us, and for three miles there was a vile compound of mud, sand, and darkness to navigate through. The moon was fairly well up in the heavens by the hour of ten o'clock, which hour saw us on the outskirts of Burlington, and we entered that beautiful little city by a splendid wide avenue, covered overhead with arching trees. According to the directions of our friend of the White Mountain House, Mr. Ferron, the Hotel Burlington was looked up, not without some difficulty, for the first place struck, the police station, could have been raided most successfully by the "Quartette," the only signs of life about it being an officer's helmet and club lying on a table in the audience-room. It being Sunday night everything was extremely quiet, scarcely a solitary citizen being seen on the streets. The " Burlington " was found after a short hunt, and leaving directions to be called for the Ausable Chasm boat, the thoroughly tired out " Quartette " turned in.

Burlington is a pretty town and a lively one in point of trade, being a great lumber centre and a port for the general transportation business done on Lakes Champlain and George.

We were up betimes on the morning following our arrival in the city, and, leaving the machines at the hotel, went on board the " Chauteaugay," plying between Burlington and the towns on the northern shores of Lake Champlain. Our destination was the Ausable Chasm and the port of landing on the New York side was Port Kent. It is about half an hour's sail across the lake, and as the green Vermont hills fell away behind us, with the city of Burlington lying below them on the shore of the magnificent sheet of water, and with a beautiful sky above us, and the hazy bluffs of the New York shore in the distance, the impression that we were in for a delightful time came home to us, and it was by no means a wrong impression, either. The monarchs of the Vermont side—Mount Mansfield

8

and the Camel's Hump—became gradually bluer and bluer as they faded into the distance, and the less picturesque shores of New York State commenced to rise higher and higher as we drew in nearer to our landing place. The distance across the lake from Burlington to Port Kent is 10 miles, and to reach the Chasm you have to go three miles by rail. The Chasm lies midway between Port Kent and Keeseville, a village on the Ausable River six miles from the lake front. About a mile and a half from Keeseville on the side of the lake the river makes a leap of about 20 feet into a semicircular pool of great beauty, and a little further down, about a mile, it takes another leap—this time of about 150 feet.

This latter waterfall is known as the Birmingham Falls. Not very far below these falls the Ausable Chasm commences. The river narrows and rushes through a channel from five to about 15 feet wide, above which rise precipices to the height of from 100 to 200 feet. The whole thing looks like a Western cañon, and the towering masses of rock inclosing the swiftly running stream impress one with the feeling that at times they are bound to fall in and crush whoever may be down in the wonderful and, in many portions, most beautiful " Royal Gorge " of New York State. All along, especially in the fissures and gorges extending on either side from the main chasm, large pieces of stone and rock lie around, where they have fallen from the overhanging cliffs, which are composed of strata which, to most people, look as though they were liable to part company and come down at any moment. These side fissures all have names, and you can scarcely go into any of the larger of them without finding hundreds of cards left by visitors who have inspected this wonderful piece of nature's handiwork. Every State in the Union is represented, and as these cards must periodically be washed or blown away, the number of people who visit the Chasm must be enormous.

The place is owned by a corporation, who charge admission and provide facilities, in the way of walks and bridges, for visitors to thoroughly inspect the wonders of the Chasm. Near where the river widens out before running into the lake, the Chasm ends. The curbed-in waters of the stream run for a distance of two miles between the precipices referred to, which sometimes are close to each other and sometimes 50 feet or more apart. Near the lower portion of the Chasm is the boat ride, which you can take or not, as you see fit.

The boat ride down what are not very dangerous rapids is a feature of the Chasm trip that is very generally patronized. You enter a large flat-bottom boat, in which are two sturdy watermen who pole and row you through the narrow part of the Chasm, where often but ten or twelve feet separate the perpendicular sides, which run up to the height of 100 feet on either hand. When about half-way through the passage, the rapids are struck, and then some care is required in the handling of the craft. You swing round this rock, and scrape over that one ; the women scream, and there is a general feeling of quiet nervousness until the boat glides into the smooth waters, where the great walls break away on each side, and the stream opens out into quiet and unconfined life. To any one who happens to be in Burlington or near it, a visit to this wonderful natural beauty of the country is well worth taking. The admission to the Chasm is 50 cents and the boat ride 50 cents additional. Take your lunch with you and spend the day there.

One of the prettiest sights at or near the Ausable Chasm is the Alice Falls, where the river takes a leap over a wide, rocky ledge, to seek a lower level before making its second descent into the Chasm at the Bir-

mingham Falls. There were several parties of tourists visiting the Chasm
as well as ourselves, and with one of them, numbering about five and
hailing from Burlington across the lake, the "Quartette" struck up quite
an acquaintance, and were treated to some inner-man comforts, and, later
in the day, on returning to Burlington, to very civil attentions on the part
of Mr. Dean B. Connell, editor of one of the city papers.

It was a beautiful morning that 21st day of July, when we left Burlington for our sail down the broad bosom of Lake Champlain. The "Vermont" is quite a large boat, and leaving Burlington in the morning at
8.30, it is scheduled to arrive at Fort Ticonderoga at 12.30 P. M. At this
place passengers take the train across the narrow neck of land separating
Lake Champlain from Lake George, and then continue their journey down
Lake George in another steamer. We did not intend to make the com-
plete trip by water, but purposed getting off at Ticonderoga and riding, if
possible, around Lake George to Caldwell, and then from there by way of
Glens Falls to Saratoga.

The "Vermont" drew out from the wharf at the appointed time, and
with the "Quartette" on the upper deck made her way into the centre of the
lake and turned her nose toward Essex and Port Henry. Champlain is
a splendid sheet of water, and while it has not the picturesque beauty of
Lake George it still has a far-stretching quiet beauty of its own which
makes it a real joy to travel on it and leaves a pleasant memory in the
mind of the traveler.

The "Quartette" sat on the upper deck and smoked, while a fresh
breeze made them feel slightly chilly.

"Here is a good opportunity for another story," said Gil; "come,
Laurie, let's hear from you."

"Don't you want to admire the scenery?" said Laurie, who looked lazy.

"Certainly we do, but that won't prevent us from listening to a good
story. Go ahead and spin your yarn; you could not have a better opportunity."

"I don't know that any story I can give you will be good, but as you
fellows seem bent on swapping lies, as the saying goes, I suppose I shall
have to do my share. What shall it be, prose or verse, tragic, comic, fish,
bicycle, love, or what?"

"Oh! Chester gave us enough sentiment to last for a twelvemonth," said
Gil; "can't you give us some fact, like that Pittsburgh election of
mine?"

"Give us some bicycling fact; you must have some incident from the
other side of the water if you have not from this," the writer ventured to
remark.

"Well, I can give you a cycling incident—a true one. Here, I have
the notes of it in this book," and Laurie drew a note-book from his
pocket. "The story was told by an Englishman in a Paris café to a half-
dozen of us when I was over there a few years ago. We were, to use the
same expression I used before, swapping lies over the convivial board
when the Englishman proposed to tell real facts, and the proposal being
agreed to he related this story, which, as a bicycler, I took an interest in
and noted down the tale almost as he told it. It is nothing extraordinary,
like Chester's narrative, and there are not the elements of local interest
about it that made Gil's story a good one, and it is not a personal experience, but it is interesting, I think, all the same."

Then, while Mt. Mansfield became an indistinct patch of blue in the
distance, and while the bright waters that had rippled round the prows of

Samuel De Champlain's birch-bark canoes curled up in front of and fell away in foam from the bow of the latter-day big steamer, on the deck of which were seated our little party, Laurie commenced his story of

## "THE CYCLER AND THE TIGER.

"I don't think you will have much of a bargain if you get me started on a true story, but since you must have it the sin be on your own head. A year ago I was stationed at Gerripore. Situated among the lower elevations of the Himalayas, this place occupies a position which in the way of climate recommends it, during a large portion of the year, to the patronage of those Europeans who find the heat of the lower portions of the great Peninsula of India extremely trying on their Caucasian make-up. As an attaché of the government engineer corps, with its then headquarters at Peshawur, I had considerable to do in the way of traveling around, and I had contrived to get from England, more as a toy than anything else, a 50-inch bicycle. It was one of the Singer make of machines and there was as good stuff and workmanship in that piece of mechanism as I have seen in any product of mechanical skill. While bicycling and tricycling are becoming popular as recreations in the immense country known as Hindoostan, still the use of these vehicles in the Empress of India's vast domain is, of course, circumscribed as compared with England, and I was only one of a bare half-dozen Europeans who within, as far as I knew, the radius of 500 miles, owned what the natives considered as a conjuror's carriage.

"This machine of which I speak, of course excited considerable attention throughout the territory that I had occasion to travel round, and on more than one occasion I took it with me when I journeyed down to Lucknow and Delhi. It was on one of these trips that I had occasion to stop at Massoree, and for the two days I was there lodged under the hospitable roof of Captain Kirby, of the ——th native infantry. The town is not a large one, and like most of these native villages it suffers every now and then at the hands of some forager of the forest, which interesting product of the country generally takes the semblance of what the outside world shudders over the thoughts of—a man-eating tiger. Of course, there are such things, but my experience of Indian life warrants me in believing that they are not nearly so numerous or so terrifying as the said outside world believes. They call them man-eaters, but if good, wholesome terror is what story-tellers want to inspire they might as well add that they are woman-eaters and child-eaters as well. In fact, I question if these same gentlemen of the forest don't prefer a plump, sleek minor human animal to a tough and well-seasoned adult. Be this as it may, the good people of this town of Massoree had been in a woeful state of fear and trembling for six months' time before I dropped among them, and all on account of the ravages of what they called the 'great man-eater.' Not satisfied with crediting him with the carrying off and masticating of two children, one woman, and three men from their own burg, they held that he was one and the same animal that had depopulated to about the same extent the village of Derbagh on the other side of the Jungle. This Jungle running close by was the *bete noir* of Massoree, and owing to its extent it offered a splendid retreat for the largest congregation of wild animals in that part of the country.

"'Mr. Nesmyth, you must not go around by yourself in the evening on the Jungle side,' said the wife of my host the day I arrived. I had mentioned something about taking a ride during the evenings, for I had my bicycle with me and Jack Kirby, Captain Kirby's son, was extremely anxious to learn to ride it.

"'Oh! I don't think there is so much to be afraid of, Mrs. Kirby,' I said, ' but, of course, if you wish it, believing all that the natives say about this striped cannibal, why, I certainly won't be rash.'

"' Well, what they say is in a great measure true, and there is really good cause for caution,' said Mrs. Kirby. ' It would never do for you to visit us to become food for even such a regal neighbor as our Bengal friend yonder.'

"'Indeed, no,' I said, laughing. ' I shall take precious good care to keep out of his clutches.'

" Now, it is a curious thing that if I had gone out hunting that tiger with all the paraphernalia considered necessary or essential to the prosecution of that royal sport of the far East, I would in all probability not have seen even the extreme tip of my four-footed friend's tail. As it was, with no desire whatever to see him—much less to see him alive and outside prison bars—I ran across that terror of the whole country side as coolly and as naturally as you please, and it happened this way :

" The outlying trees of the Jungle lay some 50 feet away from the wagon track for the distance of about half a mile, and along this stretch of rough surface I rode that evening shortly before dark. I was by myself, for cycling companions were at a premium. Well, I had reached a point about half-way past the line of brush and trees forming the outer fringe of the Jungle, when suddenly there was a rustle on my right and about 30 feet away, and about half that distance in front of me out stepped a veritable tiger. And what a tiger ! From a howdah vantage point, and with a good rifle, what a noble quarry ; but by all the gods of Hindoostan and elsewhere, what a terrible apparition viewed from the saddle of a 50-inch bicycle !

" Whether the beast had scented me and was coming after me, or whether my noiseless approach had taken him by surprise I do not know. Had he scented my moderately fat carcass, and thought that a meal off a European would go about as well as anything else, and then had presented to his eyesight an apparition that his sense of smell had not prepared him for, I knew not and cared not. All I knew was that the most magnificent tiger I had ever seen, either in or out of captivity, had come into full view and was looking at me. Up went his enormous head and then down again, the curve in his back seemed to rise several inches, there was a sweep of his majestic tail, and then with what was more of a rumbling grunt than a growl, the huge beast swung round and bounded into the bushes. Did I wait to see if he would return ? Did I ? Would you have done so ? No, gentlemen, I just did the old man Cortis act, and for half a mile imagined I heard the pat, pat of soft footsteps following the track of the bicycle. I never looked back. The animal may have followed me for a short distance, but I don't know. I do know, had any one asked me, during those terrible moments, if I would have staked my existence on that tiger being present within 50 feet of my hind wheel, for the distance of a quarter of a mile, I would have done so, for I had the feeling that he was there, though I dared not look back, and to this day I believe that, to the entrance to the village, the man-eating beast followed me, and speculated after his own peculiar fashion as to what manner of man or beast was in front of him, and whether or not he was good for food. I never heard what became of that special animal, but I suppose like nearly all of those noble beasts but terrible scourges, he fell before the rifle ball of some English sportsman. My adventure may not seem very exciting told here, but put yourselves in my place on that evening and in that company and it is an experience well enough to talk about, but not very pleasant to undergo.

" When I told my friends that night of my adventure in the early part of the evening, they were disposed to think I was giving them a good story, but on my assuring them that it was a positive truth, that I had really seen their man-eater, they did not know whether most to rejoice over my escape or envy my sight of the terror of that part of the country. Next day there was one of the periodical crusades in search of the dreaded scourge, but my friend of the previous evening had skipped. I sold my bicycle two months afterward to young Jack Kirby, who, much to his mother's terror, as I learned afterward, would sneak off for a ride in the late afternoon, with a rifle laid along the handle-bar. He never had my luck, however, in meeting the man-eater, therefore I consider that the experience is worth remembering, if it is not worth retailing in the guise of a story."

As Laurie finished his story, we drew in near Essex, on the New York shore. Here there was the usual taking on and letting off of passengers, and then in succession the boat stopped at Westport, Port Henry, Fort St. Frederick, Crown Point, with its memories of Indian, French, and English wars, and, last of all, Fort Ticonderoga, the scene of Ethan Allen's famous exploit, when in the name of the " Great Jehovah and the Continental Congress " he demanded the surrender that was agreed to by the British. At Fort Ticonderoga our water travel ended for the nonce, and recourse was again had to our bicycles. On the boat with us were a number of the Bohemian Wheelmen, of Brooklyn, N. Y. They boarded the train across to Baldwin, and took the boat at that point up Lake George to Caldwell. If we had followed their example, we would not have experienced the hardest and toughest ride of the whole trip, and would have gotten to bed, if we so wanted, in Caldwell at 8 o'clock, instead of which we rode all that afternoon, and all that night, over what they called Hague Mountain, and did not get to Bolton and to bed until one o'clock the next morning.

On leaving the steamer, as soon as the train moved off, we mounted and struck out for the town of Ticonderoga, some two or three miles distant. From this point the trend was to the right, leaving Baldwin to the left, and, after passing it, running down to the lake shore and into the little town of Hague. From the road, running along the side of the lake near this place beautiful views are obtained of the splendid sheet of water, and our cameras were several times brought into requisition. On leaving Hague the road, which in the neighborhood of Ticonderoga was terribly hard, and at Hague very fair, ran alongside the lake for some distance, and then turned to the right and went up among and over the hills. Before getting on the right road we made two mistakes, and lost the best part of an hour, which was a serious matter for us, seeing that Hague Mountain had to be crossed, and that darkness would be upon us before our stopping-place for the night could be reached. We left Ticonderoga about two o'clock, and it was between four and five when the ascent of Hague Mountain was commenced. The road was but an ordinary mountain highway, made for goats and mules, but not for bicycles, and up, up, up this ever-rising mountain road the " Quartette " manfully pushed their way. The original idea was to reach the top and ride down the other side by daylight, but darkness was already falling when we reached the crest of the mountain, and then, owing to the steepness and the roughness of the road, it was impossible to ride down that exasperating grade in the darkness. It was a case of walk and ride, ride and walk, and fall off and get on again, and then walk again.

On one occasion Gil Wiese had a narrow escape from going over the side of a bridge crossing a ravine. If he had gone over the rocky bottom of a small rivulet would have received him some 18 or 20 feet below. The road turned and twisted round and round, thank-you-ma'am after thank-you-ma'am was passed, sometimes ridden over, but more often walked, and often the road led through woods, where the only thing you could see a few yards ahead of you was the white riding-shirt of your comrade in darkness. It was a weary crowd that pulled up at the small wooden house of a laborer at the foot of the hill, and inquired how far it was to Bolton, the nearest town.

"About eight or nine miles," was the answer, and the "Quartette" went at it once more. The road was miserable, and now lay through a valley, which we judged ran down to the lake, and in this surmise we were not mistaken. Then the moon commenced to throw some light into the sky from behind the dark hills on our left, and as we skirted these hills and relegated them to the rear, the beauteous "queen of night" rose in all her glory, and gladdened our hearts with some little light. Not one of our lamps would burn, like the foolish virgins, we foolish wheelmen had not a drop of oil among the three of us.

By and by the road began to go down again, this time it is the lake sure, thought everybody. Heavy clumps of trees commenced to shut out the moonlight, but it was not long before, through the trees standing thick on our left, we could see the dancing, shimmering wavelets on Lake George. Then we ran out by the side of the glorious stretch of water, and what a view it was. Lake George by moonlight. Out in the centre of the picture could be seen the few lights yet burning at the Sagamore House, away on the far side of the lake were other lights in other hotels and on landings; above them rose the great dark hills, away in front of us lay the lights of Bolton Landing, while up in the clear heaven and slowly moving over beyond the hills the full moon threw her light over the enchanting scene. Two littly steam launches, conveying late travelers home, were out on the lake, and the singing from their occupants was borne to us as we skirted the shore and made the best of our way into Bolton, where we had to waken up the landlord at the hotel Fennimore to give us lodging for the morning.

# CHAPTER X.

### I.

Fairest Saratoga,
Brightest Saratoga,
Gayest Saratoga,
    Sing I now of thee;
Not in fair Italie,
Not in bright Arcadie,
Not in any country,
    Find I mate for thee.

### II.

O'er thee in their splendor,
Blue skies deep and tender,
To thy beauties render,
    Tribute from on high ;
Stars at night when sweeping,
O'er the heavens and keeping,
Watch above thee sleeping,
    Grieve to pass thee by.

### III.

Glorious Saratoga,
Royal Saratoga,
Grand old Saratoga,
    Here's a health to thee;
Here as faithful lover
Swear I, the world over
I cannot discover
    Spot to mate with thee.

There was not a very general movement on the part of the " Quartette " to rise betimes on the morning of July 22d. Not having crawled into bed until the morning hours, the disposition seemed to be to remain in the abode of rest until at least 12 noon had ushered us into another evening ; but there was a long ride ahead, and also, as Laurie told us, a wilderness of sand.

We were bound to make Saratoga that evening, Saratoga, that, as a late writer aptly describes it, "gayest, wickedest, and most fashionable resort of culture and refinement among watering places on this continent, if not indeed in the world." It was a ride of close on 40 miles from Bolton to Saratoga, and unless an early start were made, too much hustling would have to be indulged in to reach our goal by evening. Each one of the three grumbled fearfully when rolling out of bed, especially Gil, who had to mend his stockings again, and who was anxiously waiting for some respectable sized town where he could purchase a new pair of "Pennsylvania Grays."

What a glorious morning it was as we stepped out on the porch after breakfast. The sun shone brightly over the placid waters of the lake, reaching almost to the front entrance of the hotel. The glorious sheet of water stretching out before us in all its famed beauty, tempted a forsaking of the bicycles and a patronizing of oar and rowlock. Simultaneously we all thought of our absent Chester and his summer girl, and Laurie said :

" Well, boys, I guess we had better fight shy of boats and stick to our wheels."

Of course there was nothing else to do, and bidding good-bye to the landlord, who got our story to put in the local paper, presumably to reflect credit on his house, the "Quartette" bowled briskly along the lake road for Caldwell, 10 miles distant, at the head of the noble sheet of water. Many stops were made *en route*, to catch the beauties of the surrounding landscape, the cameras doing good service. Villa after villa was passed, and there were signs all around of the great summer population that regularly frequent this resort. As Caldwell was approached, camping parties, of which we had noted a number, commenced to grow less, and in place of white tents gleaming through the green of the trees, handsome residences, surrounded by well-kept grounds closed in on every hand, nearly all of them looking out on the "Silvery Water," which is the correct translation of the musical name of Lake Horican, by which Lake George is known in the glowing pages of Fenimore Cooper. The old French name of this "Queen of American Waters" is also a beautiful and suggestive one—*Lac Du St. Sacrament*, the "Lake of the Blessed Sacrament"—so named by the Jesuit Father Jogues, who, the first white man to gaze upon its beauties, was carried across it in 1642 a maimed and tortured prisoner, by his captors, the ruthless Iroquois Indians. Escaping from their stronghold by the aid of some friendly Indians, this self-sacrificing apostle of Christianity and civilization returned to France, but four years later, the year 1646, found him again among the North American Indians. It was in this year he gave the lake the name which it bore for a hundred years, and then surrendered up his life to the savage Mohawks. In 1755 General Johnson re-christened it "Lake George," in honor of the then reigning King of Great Britain.

The road from Bolton to Caldwell is a good one, and is kept in condition by the various hotels and resorts along the lake front. It skirts the lake almost the entire distance between the two rivers. Nothing extraordinary being characteristic of Caldwell, a stop was not indulged in, but the direct road was taken and followed at a brisk gait to Glens Falls. From Caldwell to Glens Falls, a distance of about eight miles, there is a plank road, and it forms for the entire distance remarkably good riding. The approach to Glens Falls, which is quite a manufacturing place, is very pleasing. You descend a long grade, going down which a good view is obtained of the town. At Glens Falls lunch was in order, and then, with many misgivings, the direct road to Saratoga was taken. It is about 18 miles from Glens Falls to Saratoga, and that our misgivings touching the road were justified is fully shown by the fact that we walked 11 out of the 17 or 18 miles which should have been ridden. Cyclers will find it to their advantage to take the more circuitous route by way of Fort Edward, for, if they do as we did, take the direct road running from Glens Falls to Saratoga, they had better study up the literature of expletives before they embark on the enterprise. The road for 11 miles is simply unrideable, and as for that distance there are practically no side-paths the state of our case can be very well imagined. Although not quite as tired as on the former day's trip over the Lake George hills, the "Quartette" returned heartfelt thanks when that road, fearfully and wonderfully made, or rather not made at all, faded away behind, and the light and life and wealth of Saratoga closed around us as we made our way to the Commercial Hotel. That night we did the Springs, and the fine string band at Congress Hall Park had to stand a fire of criticism from those short-breeched travelers who had not been treated to such sweet sounds for several weeks.

Saratoga is a collection of mammoth hotels. No conception can be had

9

of the number and size of these great hostelries without actually seeing them. And what a blaze of beauty and fashion these hotels present at night when under the glare of the electrics. "Greek meets Greek" in the mad whirl that is born of the possession of intellect, money, and passion. At Saratoga you can take your medicine in any fashion you may desire. If you are ordered to drink the waters you have your choice of dozens of springs, all boasting their marvelous properties and all the "best." If you are visiting the place for a restful time, you can have a restful time, with the most lovely surroundings to militate to your comfort. If you want a gay time that is the place to have it. If you look for a religious time you can enjoy it there as well as anywhere else. The young debutante with a fortune can there find, very likely, a matrimonial companion with another fortune, or with perhaps a title. The aspiring young blood from Broadway and Fifth Avenue, to quote the words of Trevelyan on Charles James Fox, there finds himself "surrounded with every facility for ruining himself with the least delay and in the best company." If you are a sportsman you have thrown at your feet that glorious elysium of wood and water that makes Northern New York State the "Mecca" of so many worn-out workers in our vast centres of commercial strife and enterprise. Truly, Saratoga would have suited those "men of Athens" who delighted ever in some "new thing."

Saratoga, the cosmopolitan, is the sobriquet most aptly describing this world-famous resort. The "Quartette" spent one evening and half a day noting the sights, and at 2 o'clock Thursday afternoon, after a hearty meal, pulled out from the great watering place, and took the road to Albany via Dunning Street, Mechanicsville, and Troy. The road out of Saratoga was fair, but there had been several heavy showers of rain during the previous night, and off and on during the forenoon, with a probability of others, and the road surface had suffered considerably in consequence. Mud predominated for about five miles, and as clay constituted a considerable portion of the ingredient of which the said surface was composed, riding became very heavy. By the side of Round Lake the party tumbled into what was a regular "Slough of Despond" on the side of a short hill. This was one of the most curious experiences of the trip. The order of march was Roberts, Wiese, and the writer. Looking at this hill from the top, rapid transit over its surface appeared practicable, and "Forward the Light Brigade," in the person of Roberts was the programme. After him went Gil, the heavy man of the party, and then the writer. Well! that hill was simply a mud hole. Laurie got through to the bottom on his wheel and then fell off on a comparatively hard spot. Gilbert got half way and then his wheel choked with mud, threw him into the filthy compound, which at that precise spot enveloped his manly proportions to the knees, and nearly all the way to the right hip. Scared by what was going on in front, the writer did not wait to try conclusions with the middle of the grade, but twisting to one side and carrying a bucketful of mud on wheels and frame, fell in a rank growth of green weeds and bushes by the side of the roadway. "Sure such a sight was never seen" before or since by the participants. The two machines had to be lifted bodily up the side bank, for the wheels refused to revolve, and then a stick was cut from a neighboring bush and a surgical operation commenced to relieve an abnormal growth in their proportions. Beyond this point the road for several miles proved soft, and then as the evening closed down, it most fortunately turned into a slate macadam highway, and at a rattling gait the "Quartette" rolled into the busy, bustling town of Mechanicsville.

There was every prospect that more rain would fall during the night, and this was most annoying, seeing that the worst roads had been covered and for the short remaining distance to Albany, a well-surfaced pike extended, which could be easily covered in the morning, in time to get the day boat down the great and glorious Hudson for New York.

The "Talmadge," the house of entertainment at which we stopped in Mechanicsville, was one of the coziest and most comfortable which we had struck on our travels, and the fact that we were extremely well treated was no doubt in part due to the hotel being a favorite stopping-place for cyclers. We were not aware of this when deciding to put up there, but soon found that we had not made any mistake in choosing our lodgings. The hotel is on the direct road to Troy and Albany, and as this road is one of the best in that part of the State, it is much patronized by wheelmen.

"Laurie, you ought to be ashamed of yourself," said Gil, when sitting in the parlor after supper.

"Well! I like that. It seems to me you are the one to be ashamed of yourself. Why don't you clean your machine?"

"The thoughts of great minds run in the same channel. The saying must be a true one, my remark was caused by my thinking you rode the most disreputably dirty bicycle I ever laid eyes on," said Gil.

"Let's both jump on Mac then, we won't ride with him to-morrow unless he cleans up," replied the owner of unfortunate machine No. 1.

"Well," said Gil, "we will say nothing about the matter, though that old wooden cart of his does look tough, if he tells us that story he owes. We have all, as you put it, Laurie, 'swapped lies,' except the rider of the hardest looking wheel in the crowd."

"I don't feel any more like telling a story than I feel like cleaning a wheel," ventured the writer, and then added, "suppose we put the stable man to work."

"That's a good idea, more especially if we have to train it to-morrow morning, as now appears likely," said Gil.

The rain was falling heavily as we crossed the yard to the coach-house, and as everything pointed to our having to sample the railroad for the short run into Albany the next morning, the stableman was made happy by the opportunity to earn an honest penny currying our rubber-hoofed steeds.

On returning to the hotel Laurie again proposed to have the "Quartette's" fourth story, but on representing that the long trip down the Hudson might be a little more tedious than would be the retailing of the said story, it was agreed to postpone its recital until the following day.

After a conference as to the advisability of riding to Albany next morning, the decision was arrived at to ride if the rain ceased. If the inclement weather continued, then, for the sake of sentiment, it would be nonsense to cover the few miles awheel, and recourse to the railroad would be the sensible programme. Leaving word to be called at four o'clock, if no rain was falling, the party divided up into singles to, first, pray for a fine morning, and then sleep for a longer time than had been our lot for a week before.

Whether the "Quartette" did not stand very high in the favor of Heaven, or whether the prayers above referred to were too short or not wide-awake enough, four o'clock the next morning saw the rain still falling heavily, and Gilbert was recreant enough to say that he was glad of the chance for a longer sleep than he had expected.

The distance from the hotel to the railroad station was about a quarter of a mile, and under the steady down-pour the three of us ran "a-muck," in a double sense, over the foot pavements to the D. & H. C. Co.'s depot. A few rain-drops and all blue-coated representatives of the law were dodged successfully, and the last machine lifted into the baggage car with the assistance of an obliging hack driver, just as the train moved off. In the hurry attending the getting of the machines on board, Laurie cut his hand severely, and a handkerchief was scarcely large enough to form an effective bandage. By the time we had made the Hudson trip, however, and with the aid of a roll of court-plaster, the wounded member was again in trim for riding.

Seen from the car windows as the train ran down to Albany, a good view was had of the road which we would have ridden over but for adverse circumstances. It appeared a first-class one, but as then seen had an uninviting top-dressing of mud, with numerous small puddles into which the rain-drops splashed dismally.

"Boys, if good old Charlie Harvey were with the 'Quartette,' ten chances to one but we would be riding along out there getting our faces washed," said Laurie.

"You bet I wouldn't," put in Gil. "I like to ride in trains as little as anybody, but excuse me from fun that's no fun, as Mac might say."

It took but a few minutes to make the run to Albany, passing *en route*, the busy centres of Troy and West Troy, and then, skirting the immense aggregation of lumber along the far-reaching docks of the Delaware and Hudson Canal Co., the train brought us up beside the wharf where lay the big boat that was to bear us down the Hudson. The rain slackened just then, and there was promise overhead for a clear day after all.

" No charge for bicycles, put them along in that gangway," were the words of the deck officer, as we got aboard, and in two minutes' time the wheels were stowed and things began to take on a brighter hue as the rain ceased and the big steamer drew away from the wharf.

Albany presents a pleasing appearance viewed from the river, the much-talked-about Capitol building, showing up to advantage above the many other large edifices of the city. From the distant view obtained of it, this much-lauded architectural creation seemed to us as not being anything near what the City Hall of Philadelphia is, so far as exterior appearance goes, although it may be perfectly true that, as regarding its interior fittings, it is without a rival in this country.

At Albany the Hudson is an unpretentious and an uninteresting stream giving but scant promise of the beauties which further down make it world, famed for its scenery. Securing seats on the middle deck, the "Quartette" made itself comfortable, Gil being in the "seventh heaven" of satisfaction, because there was a band on board. Music is one of the big factors of day and night travel on the Hudson, a brass and string band being attached to every boat plying between New York and Albany.

" Boys, we're in for a nice trip, there is a patch of blue sky yonder and there goes the music," said our crank on the subject of sweet sounds, as our boat, the "City of New York," swung loose from her berth and commenced to make her way carefully down-stream. The spires, roofs, and chimneys of Albany, dropped behind, soon a couple of bends in the. river shut them out from view, and then as the stream broadened, the steamer began to make the time for which the Hudson River boats are noted. Comfortably ensconced on the middle deck, close to the musicians where we had located ourselves to please Gil, there was nothing to do but chat, smoke, and take note of our fellow-passengers. As is always the case, there was quite a crowd on board, embracing all sorts and conditions of men and women. Rich, poor, business people, pleasure seekers, and the ubiquitous loafer. There were quite a number of parties going on, or returning from summer trips among the many places of interest through which the Hudson runs as the main artery of travel. From Lake George and its surrounding beauty spots, from Saratoga, from the Adirondacks and the hundred and one other places easily reached from the upper waters of this noble stream, the palace steamer was carrying away crowds of pleasure seekers, whose places would immediately be filled by number-less others, and so the great tide of summer travel goes on all through the season, and when the name of the Hudson River is brought up, wherever a little knot of American travelers are gathered, it generally recalls pleasurable reminiscences to a number of them.

About an hour's time was filled in after this fashion, and, when the novelty of the music had worn off, and the immediate surroundings had been fairly well sized up, Laurie moved for an adjournment to the upper deck for a more extended view and for the telling of the last story.

"This is Friday, boys," he said, "to-night we may not feel like sitting up, and to-morrow we will have to ride clear across New Jersey. So let's have Mac's story."

"Yes, go ahead, as we are on the water we want a yarn," chimed in Gil.

It was the writer's turn to spin the bargained-for tale, so he asked the question :

"Well, boys, what will you have ?"

"I never take anything stronger than beer, and very little of that," exclaimed Gil.

"It is very little of that you will get just now, except you are disposed to do the paying. What I asked you about was how you wanted to be treated in the way of a story ? What kind do you fellows want ?"

"Any kind," said Laurie ; "make it about the boys, the girls, or bicycles, but preferably let the ingredients be the two former, as we are well-versed in matters regarding the latter, thanks to the past three weeks."

"Amen," came seriously from Gil.

"Well, then, here goes, boys, let's have what we will call the story of

## ANNETTE.

### CHAPTER I.

"Annette, I love you."

I whispered the words in her ear, she was the last one to whom I was bidding farewell on the pier, and then I sprang from her side, and crossing the gang-plank stood upon the deck of the "Aurania."

I was the last passenger to board the great Atlantic liner, and as I reached the deck, I turned to look back at, and shout to, the knot of re-latives and friends who had come down to the pier to see me off for Europe.

Annette Lascelles was among them. I loved Annette, but never had had the courage to confess the fact to her until then, then, a half-second, which I felt with a lover's instinct was my own and hers, gave me the sudden inspiration to make known that love under what must have been the most curious circumstances that ever enamored swain could have chosen for such a confession.

The moment I gained the deck and turned to look back, my eye sought out Annette. She was staring after me with more of a look of blank amazement upon her face than anything else, there was a flush on her cheek and the hand she had suddenly placed on Cousin Bess' arm I fancied was used to steady herself. I waved my hand and then threw a kiss which I meant individually of course, but which was taken collectively. Only a few yards separated us from the pier, and the big boat had just commenced lazily to drift out under surveillance of the tugs. " Goodbye, *au revoir*," I shouted.

" I'll not forget the cane, Jack," I said to my brother, as I leaned over the rail.

" Nor my fur cape," said Cousin Bess.

" Don't forget the Pneumatic," shouted my younger brother, Dave.

" What shall I buy you, Annette," I called out. " A diamond—" ring I was about to say, but she interpolated, as quick as a flash :

" Necklace—a diamond necklace," while the rest of the party laughed, and Cousin Bess said something to her, and I thought I could see her color heighten again.

Then she drew out a dainty, little, pink-edged handkerchief, and waved it to me, while the big vessel forged slowly into the stream.

I devoutly wished then that I knew the deaf and dumb alphabet and that she knew it, or else that I was conversant with some nautical or other signal code and that she had studied the same code to advantage, so that I could ask one question and get an answer one way or the other, but there I stood like a big fool, waving my handkerchief it was to be presumed to a group of 20 persons, when in reality I was thinking only about one, and for all I knew without one iota of any sort of encouragement to keep on thinking of her. But there she stood, and the pink-edged handkerchief kept on waving as long as I could make out the special little crowd, and the special trim-built little figure that was to me the embodiment of all the prettiness, piquancy, and goodness of the femininity of New York.

" Confound my irresolution !" I muttered, and then I turned to watch Bartholdi's colossal Statue of Liberty loom up ahead, as we slowly made our way down the bay.

### CHAPTER II.

Mid ocean.

Have you ever lost yourself in a sea of speculation, and, utterly bewildered, given up ? Tossing around, grasping after something intangible, have returned to the landmarks of sober reason, and then taken up again one of the more sensible themes or duties of every-day life, to find in it more true enjoyment than could be found in all the wild experimenting with unknown quantities ?

Have you ever crossed the—wide I was going to say, but it is wide no longer—stretch of water between America and Europe, and while in mid ocean, with nothing but the sea and sky around you, nothing outside the plates of iron that intervene between you and one of the most pitiless of elements, but other elements equally as pitiless when roused to wrath by one of their number trespassing on the territory of the others ? While thus situated, I repeat, have you ever dreamed ?

If you have not, you have no business on the vasty deep. You have no business there except to be sick, and as near sick unto death as it is possible to be, for that should be the only excuse for a mortal, blessed as the case may be, with or without imagination, not dreaming whether he be old or young. He must dream when he finds himself flung, as it were, more closely under the eye of Heaven than he can possibly find himself anywhere else on earth, except perhaps, on the wide expanse of some Westernland prairie.

Breasting the green billows under somewhat such circumstances as those which may have drawn from William Allingham the well-known lines:

> "A wet sheet and a flowing sea
> And a wind that follows fast,"

only steam instead of poetic air was her motive power, the good ship "Aurania" plunged on into the nearer Orient, and leaning back on the securely-lashed steamer chair, watching the blue smoke from the half-consumed cigar between my lips curl up toward the bluer vault above, I dreamed.

Boys, do you care for dreams?

Sometimes they are worth listening to, sometimes they are not. Sometimes, for the mere reason that they are dreams, they possess a fascination altogether wanting in the more practical phases of what is a most practical thing, life, only equalled in point of practicalness by one other thing, death; and the practicalness of the latter, so far as we are concerned as individuals, is limited, so to speak, to the speculative, for our experience of it will be so eminently practical that we can but leave to others a legacy of the speculations we at one time indulged in ourselves regarding it.

But we are wandering, and what wonder; nay, rather, we are commencing to dream, and what more natural, with naught but sky above us, naught but water round us, nothing to take the place of wind whisperings through the leaves of many trees but ever and anon discordant sighings of the wayward breeze round ropes and lines of various thicknesses and different powers of resistance. Further, nothing between us and the speculatively practical save a quarter of an inch or maybe a half-inch of metal. But we don't think of this latter fact; it is the farthest off of any from our thoughts, we give no heed to it, we dream, and then we dream again; and then—well, what follows is to come.

#### CHAPTER III.

I loved Annette.

I had loved her from the first moment I had set eyes upon her, or rather from the first moment my eyes met hers on the night the Wrexhams gave the ball that was a nine days' wonder of Fifth Avenue, and which is now, except in cases such as my own, not more than a half memory.

Annette was not handsome, she was pretty. I did not want her to be handsome, or, rather, to me she was handsome, more handsome than the proudest beauty, product of royal court or Imperial palace, and I have seen a great many such lights of the social world—that is, I have been privileged, as the "old world" citizen would put it, to look upon them.

Did Annette love me? Dolt that I was, I had not discovered whether she did or not. I had paid her the most marked attention, and she was the sweetest little friend that man could have; but strange, with her I felt a diffidence that, truth to tell, was scarcely characteristic of me in a general sense, and unlike the brave, whose right the old saying has it is to deserve the fair, by my hesitancy and procrastination I most certainly did not deserve the wave of that pink edged handkerchief that was my only answer, to the desperately and hotly-breathed words: "Annette, I love you."

Heavens! I, calling myself a man, afraid to speak to a little mite of a weak woman, and taking a boy's method of confessing what might be a fault, when I knew I was pretty safe to escape immediate punishment. But, the pink-edged taste of muslin or what ever it was, as small and delicate, as prim and pretty as its owner; did its fluttering to the breeze that flounced out from the heights of Hoboken mean anything?

Pshaw! I flung the cigar overboard and sprang to my feet, and the deck did not slope sufficiently to divert my nervous tread more than a few planks one way or other as I strode rapidly from one end of the promenade-deck to the other.

If Tom Campbell is to be trusted in regard to his assertion that "distance lends enchantment to the view," then he solves the problem of how it came about that as knot after knot was reeled off by the stout ship bearing me away from the now far-off Western World, the view in my mind's eye of that dingy New York pier, with its commonplace surroundings remained the most interesting spo' among the many I had knowledge of in the great land that owned me as a son, and the one little object that was the head and front of that bright mind's-eye vista grew into a tantalizing concentration of enchantment that was positively unnerving.

"Confound it!" I said, "there is no such thing as stopping off here, changing cars, side-tracking, or doing as the wise men are said to do, taking second thought and in my case going back. What did you go away for anyhow, Will Chaytor?"

What had I gone away for anyhow?

I had asked myself the question, and hardly knew how to answer it. The only answer I could make was: For pleasure.

And here I was, fretting to be back once more. Clearly I was not on a trip of pleasure bound. I might have dreamed of taking such a trip, but the dream was certaiuly in a very poor way of being realized.

I crossed to the rail and leaned over, watching the waters apparently travel by at racing speed. I only looked for a moment. It annoyed me to see the demonstrating evidence that I was getting farther and farther away from the place that now I wished the less and less to be removed from.

"Will Chaytor, you are a fool," I said, as I threw myself down once more in my chair. The blue vault above looked as deep and beautiful— well, as deep and beautiful as Annette's eyes. "Will Chaytor, you are a fool," I repeated, and drew a big rug closely round me while the brisk wind blowing from the far-off American shore seemed to throw back to me as an echo the words: "Will Chaytor, you are a fool!"

The breeze was but a poor comforter, it would make savage attacks on the end of the rug, it would insist on trying to tear my cap off, and the blue sky above looked down as deep and beautiful as—confound it, I could not help making the comparison again—as deep and beautiful as Annette's eyes.

I made a rush for the library and pulling from a row of George Sand's works the volume *Consuelo*, strove to bury my thoughts in those of another.

### CHAPTER IV.

Six days out.

We were off the Irish Coast. Every eye was strained to catch the first glimpse of the Fastnet Rock, with the famous lighthouse dominating its rugged and storm-beaten sides. The possessors of the numerous field glasses trained on the Eastern horizon were the first ones to shout, "I see it, there it is."

"Where is it? let me look, please let me look," and many such words dropped from rosy lips under sunburnt cheeks, and from pale blue lips under as pallid sick-lined faces.

I was not looking toward the Fastnet, I had seen it before, and, moreover, I had not been sea-sick, though I had not been enjoying myself to any extraordinary extent. I was looking astern, to where, in the distance, the great white wake of the steamer melted into the green-blue of water and sky, and watching the fading West, where the sun was fast dropping down to rest. In an hour we were up to the sentinel of gray rock that guards the first approach to the European Continent on the main route across the Atlantic. We were past it, the flag had been raised and lowered by the watchers on that lone ocean post, ours had been run up also, and I knew that within a few moments, over the wires would be flashing the news to the "Old World" and the "New World" alike, that the good ship "Aurania" had arrived.

Would Annette scan the paper in the morning to see if I had reached port safely, would she give more than a passing thought to the fact that I had? Would she feel any more than the ordinary satisfaction of a friend who learns that a friend had safely completed a journey on which the danger of accident was a probability?

I could not help such thoughts. Then as the red sun sank away in that far West where lay my thoughts, and as the crimson streaks of what was a glorious sunset shot up among the higher clouds, I turned to look on the gray shores looming up on our left. I wished it were morning instead of evening; I did not like the great shadows falling over the rocky coast and the distant inland heights of Kerry and Clare. I had seen them under the glancing sunlight, and they had looked bright and fair, but as night closed down they appeared dark and forbidding, and even the bright full moon slowly rising and welcoming us ocean sojourners to her "Old World" realm, failed to rouse me to an appreciation of the beauties of Queenstown Harbor on a clear, bright night. I marked the round topped hills as we ran through by the forts; they were familiar objects. I marked the odd lights twinkling up above the ramparts, showing that life was there. Then across the glistening waters of the harbor, other lights from the white-fronted houses of the town came into view as we swung out from where the anchor dropped below the silver-tipped waves. Then the lights seemed to creep behind the black hull and square yards of a huge British man-of-war, but of course they were stationary and it was we who were swinging round with the tide. Then came the assault from the shore and I was watching a big Irishman trying to sell one of my traveling companions a blackthorn stick for double its value, when somebody touched me on the arm, and looking round I saw our table steward, who surprised me by saying,

"There is a telegram for you in the saloon, sir."

I thanked him, and not waiting to see the result of the deal over the blackthorn, went down the companion-way.

Who could be telegraphing me? I expected one or two letters from London, but had not looked for a wire from either side of the Atlantic, and I wondered if anything unexpected could have happened at home, or if anything extraordinary had transpired among my friends in England.

On the table in the saloon were two letters addressed to me and a message. It was a cable, and from America. I allowed the letters to lie and hastily tore open the message and read it. Then I read it a second time, I even read it a third time. Then I laid it on the table and sat down and

10

looked at it. Then I got up again, held it to the light, I could not doubt it. The words were there and they were these :

" Will Chaytor, you are a fool to leave New York and Annette."

" Boys, I'm hungry," broke in Gil Wiese, "and it's lunch-time ; there is a dining-room aboard and Mac's sentiment has shut his ears without opening his eyes."

" Can't you wait awhile longer and hear the finish of the story ?" said Laurie.

" Not when I have heard the dinner bell," said Gil; " come along, eat first and talk afterward."

It was Gil's style. You could not do anything with him. Put him in Westminster Abbey near lunch-time, and he would not take a guide-book in one hand unless you put a ham sandwich or something better in the other. The writer must plead guilty to being perfectly willing that the practical member of the party should be the puller of chestnuts out of the fire. He would also when hungry sooner eat than tell stories, and Laurie, who was beginning to think his brother's story all right, thus left hopelessly in the minority, gracefully gave in, and the three pairs of knickerbockers, sailing down the "Knickerbocker " stream, on the pre-eminently " Knicker-bocker " boat, turned into the big dining saloon of the " New York," and secured a table to themselves.

" Do you know what a story always seems like to me, whether I read it or hear it told ?" said Gil, as the soup appeared.

Not getting any reply, he went on.

" It seems like this plate of soup ; you don't know what's in it."

We all looked up, while the darkey waiter looked down, and with a be-nignant countenance remarked :

" That is mullagatawny, sir."

" Ah, I didn't mean what was in the plate," said Gil ; " I meant what was in the soup."

The countenance of the dusky attendant did not smile quite as much on hearing this, and he went after a spoon.

" Gil, you will get us all in the soup if you talk like that," put in Laurie.

" You're not dipping into a well, Gil, but you may find the truth you are looking for at the bottom of that plate," said the writer.

" Well, if I do find this particular soup, pure and undefiled mullagatawny, I will retract and say it is unlike a story."

" Rather rough on yourself, Gil, as well as on Pittsburgh."

" Not a bit of it. I'll prove the truth of my story, which is an exception to the general run. But you fellows can't shove on me your Lake George vagaries, or the stories of your being chased by tigers in India, or chasing yourselves for no reason whatever across the ocean. Oh ! no, but I'm curious to know what MacOwen did with that New York product of sweetness."

" You don't mean to say you think I'm relating a personal experience, Gil !" almost shouted the writer.

" Why of course I do. You told the thing that way, so you need not get mad, anyhow if you were not ' in it ' so much the worse luck for you, and it's only another proof of what I said about truth in most stories being an unknown quantity."

" Well I'm very sorry to spoil your idea, I am not the hero, but I know him and can vouch for the truth of the story which of course I tell in my own words."

" Oh! use whatever words you like—only don't let them be quite as tough as this duck—I wish I had taken roast beef—anyhow, Mac, what did the fellow do about the telegram ?"

" I protest against having our last romance spoiled by the contiguity of tough duck, it is bad enough, Gil, to have a ' doubting Thomas ' like yourself around. Wait until we go on deck," remarked Laurie.

In half an hour's time we were once more enjoying the delights of pure air and a wide vista from the upper deck, and as the interesting portion of the trip lay further down-stream the interrupted story was in order.

" Come now, give us the rest of Annette, and don't hurry, for we have a good stretch of the river before us," said Laurie.

Gil settled himself to listen with an evident air of interest, and the big steamer and the tale voyaged on.

## CHAPTER V.

" Will Chaytor, you are a fool."

The condemnation which I had passed upon myself, receiving such a swift and indisputable confirmation, and that, too, from a quarter whence I had least expected it, was nearly the last straw, which, according to the old saying, is bound to break the camel's back.

What did it all mean ? Did the words staring me in the face, or more correctly speaking, the words at which I was staring, signify that I had hopelessly and irrevocably hurt myself in the estimation of Annette, or, on the contrary, were they intended to convey the impression to me that Annette thought sufficiently of me to be pleased at my bold confession at the moment of leaving, while being displeased at my going away from all that I professed to hold dearest. Never in my school-boy days had I to wrestle with a proposition in Euclid or an obstinate algebraic equation so desperately as I had to work over the problem as to what that telegram meant. Why was it sent ? what mission was it designed to perform ? what should I do about it ?

I realized the truth that on my action depended what was more to me then, than the acquisition of the world's empire would have been to an Alexander or a Napoleon. That message meant something. It meant one of two things, either that Annette meant to be my friend or that she was something more.

## CHAPTER VI.

The return trail.

I had resolved to take it, and I held in my hand the schedule of Western sailings of the ocean greyhounds. For one-half hour I pondered over the import of the message and then my resolve was taken. I will accept the words, " Will Chaytor, you are a fool to leave New York and Annette," as a command to return from the " Old World " and all that it offered in the way of pleasure, the friends who were expecting me there, the acquaintances of many a bright memory of the past, the boon companions who were looking for my coming to duplicate in a milder way the frolics of old times. I would throw them all to the four winds, if I could find but a favoring breeze to bear me on the return trail across " old ocean," as fast, or faster than I had come over it.

It was Saturday. By consulting the table of sailings and interviewing the first officer, I found that I could catch one of the flyers the next day at Queenstown if I got off there instead of going on to Liverpool. It took me but an instant to decide upon this, once my mind was made up as to how I should accept the meaning of Annette's message, and, grip in hand,

I bade a hasty farewell to my shipmates, who wondered at my sudden determination to go ashore at the Irish port, and after a few minutes' dash across the bright waters of Queenstown Harbor, I stood upon the landing and ran the gauntlet of the customs authorities. Then, suddenly, the thought came to me, how about those remembrances for the family, how about that necklace for Annette. I must get them, and surely Cork, a few miles up the river Lee, must be enough of a city to possess a fur cape, and even the necklace for Annette. Happy thought, those pneumatic bicycles just come out, and one of which my younger brother had desired me to bring him, were a product of the very island I was in, there must be an agent for them in the capital of Munster

By rail to Cork was but a pins-head of travel, and a fur cape was assured of a trip across the ocean. An Irish blackthorn stick and a bog oak cane joined the cape, and then I went for the biggest jeweler in the city. Before I found him I ran across the agency for the Mecredy cycles, with pneumatic tires, and that job was settled, but here my luck stopped. I could not get a necklace to suit. In the whole of Cork I could not find one good enough for Annette, and then another thing cropped up, which, strange to say, I had not thought of before. I had not enough money with me. My letter of credit was all I had, beyond what I had spent on my other purchases.

What was I to do? Wait for the next steamer or forfeit the present for Annette, the most important gift of the lot? What action would Annette think most of, my prompt return minus the necklace, or a later arrival with the most beautiful gift I could find in the line of diamonds? It did not take long for me to decide that I would return by the very next boat, even if I had to forego the bearing of a costly token of love from the shores of the "Old World" to the shores of that other "New World" which held Annette.

But stay, no need to lose the chances that the bearing of the necklace might give me. There was a way yet as certainly as there was a will. I went to the branch of the National bank in the city, stated my case partially to the cashier, and in half an hour the wires carried a message to one of the largest exporting houses in Liverpool, to whom I was well known, saying to secure one of the finest diamond necklaces in the city of Liverpool, and send it by special messenger via Holyhead and Dublin to catch the "Servia" the next day at Queenstown. A second telegram sent personally, and partly explaining matters, and placing limit of price at £500, with orders to draw on New York for that amount, followed the first one.

I knew that, providing the message reached our house in Liverpool in time, they would attend to the business without questioning. They were aware I was on the "Aurania," and while they might wonder at what looked like some vagary on my part, they could not afford to do anything but follow my orders. The matter then was so far settled until I could get an answer from them by return wire. In due course it came, and read, "Messenger leaves this P. M. on the 'Servia' with goods as directed."

My head felt light as I walked away from the bank and sought my hotel. That night I slept as solidly as any rock lying a hundred fathoms below the reach of wind and tide, for the next night I knew would see me 100 miles west of the Fastnet on the return trail over "old ocean."

# CHAPTER VII.

All aboard!

All were aboard the big ocean liner. The tender which had brought off the Queenstown passengers lay alongside the long black hull of the "Servia." She looked by contrast like a forester's cottage set down by some Rhine fortress, or like a New England frame homestead dropped beside a Chicago monolith of brick and mortar.

"Sign here, sir," said a smooth-faced ministerial-looking individual, wearing the whitest linen, the smallest black tie, and the neatest check suit I had seen since leaving New York.

He was the representative of the firm I had wired to in Liverpool, and he had put into my hands the small package, which, opened before him, contained a box holding what was a superb necklace.

I signed the paper that he laid before me, which was a receipt for the valuable consignment, and thanked him for the attention.

"I suppose you are aware that the article is dutiable," he said, looking up at me.

"Yes, I guess it will cost me something to cross the gangway with it at New York," I replied.

"Not necessarily so," he said.

As he folded up the paper I noticed the sparkle of a diamond ring which he wore on the fourth finger of his left hand.

"I see you are a judge of good stones," I said, as my eye dwelt on the brilliant in its rich setting.

He raised his finger to the light and turned the ring round with the fingers of his other hand, saying,

"Yes, it is a very fair stone; I gave £50 for it yesterday."

I looked at it a moment and then said,

"I want just such a ring as that. I will give you £60 for it."

He took the ring from his finger. I paid him the money, and, apparently thinking that he had had a pleasant trip, if a short one, he boarded the tender and joined the group on her deck, who were waving handkerchiefs and shouting to us as we weighed anchor and headed out of the harbor. The package, with a few other things I placed in care of the purser, and under the slanting rays of the western dropping sun we steamed out between the forts and ran along the same coast which I had passed but little over a day before. The green round-topped hills faded away behind us. The bright sunlight seemed to come to meet us from the western sky, the heavy swells of the great Atlantic came broader and longer as we edged slowly away from the leeward shore. Once more the "Fastnet" loomed up, this time on our right. Once more the flags waved and once more the wires bore the message that the good ship "Servia" was on the westward trail, and I was happy. Would Annette's eye note the sailing? If so, would she have the remotest idea that I was on board? Impossible! It would be the last thing she would think of. It would be the last thing that any one in New York would think of. She might half expect a letter, but a letter could not reach New York before I would once more set foot on the pier, or the next pier to the one on which I had left her. I was happy.

# CHAPTER VIII.

Homeward bound.

Yes, homeward bound, and homeward bound meant Annette. Stay, did it mean Annette? What reason had I to believe that it did? I did

not know. I do not know now why I felt that there was not a doubt
ahead. There might be 3,000 miles of water, there might be storm and
tempest, there might be danger, even death. I did not think of any of
them. I only thought of Annette, and as I stood on the forward deck and
saw the heavy rolling seas part to right and left before the prow of the huge
mass of steel and iron bearing me into the red lap of the western sky, I
only thought of one bright spot in the world of golden light flung over the
sea and sky in front of me, and that one bright spot was the dingy pier
on the North River where I had last seen Annette.

CHAPTER IX.

Six days out.
We were past the "Banks." The ocean breeze had given place to a
few hours of fog. The business-like roll of the dark billows of the Atlantic, melting into the long, easy, lighter green swell of the "Banks,"
had given place to a somewhat heavier sea, and the great ship rolled
slightly as she bore down on the eastern shore of the New World.
Again I lay on that same steamer chair. Again the same wind seemed
to dislike that my rug should be rolled so tightly round me, again it strove
to play fast and loose with the cap which I had pulled securely down over
my ears. Again the blue curls of smoke from one of my last cigars floated
away to that other blue above, that blue which had made me think of Annette's eyes, and which now made me think of them again, and again I
dreamed.
I will ask you again, boys, do you care for dreams?
You do; well, here is what I dreamed.
It seemed as though we were already passing underneath the uplifted
hand of the Bartholdi statue in New York Bay. Then we had passed
Quarantine without a stop, and then, running by the Battery and leaving
the square tower of the Produce Exchange and the tapering spire of old
Trinity Church behind, we dropped into our berth alongside the pier.
Among the crowds on the pier I eagerly sought for some one whom I
might know. Suddenly my eye caught sight of a little group standing
apart from the body of the crowd, and my heart jumped as I recognized
the familiar faces of those who had seen me off from the same place but
two short weeks previous. I could not believe my eyes. Not one or two
or three were there, but all of them. All of them, did I say? Not all of
them. I looked again. Most surely not all of them were there. Where
was—was—was Annette? I rubbed my eyes and looked again. Yes,
they were all there, Annette must be there, she must be. But look as I
might, as hard and as long as I could, there was no Annette, there was no
wave of a pink-edged handkerchief, there was no leaning of a little figure
on a larger and stronger one, there was no—confound it! everything was
dark and misty, there was no light, and then a most diabolical pandemo-
nium of laughter commenced, which died away as I awoke into the re-
verberations of the dinner gong and the human merriment of a number of
my fellow-travelers who were standing round me when I had rolled off
my chair to the deck.
"Hallo, Chaytor," said one of them. "You were having a sweet old
time there to yourself. You've burnt a hole in your rug; what on earth
were you dreaming about?"
"I would wager from the way you look, Mr. Chaytor, that you dreamed
you lost the pool on to-day's run, which you were so sure of winning a half
hour back," said another.

"I was not dreaming at all," I said, "I was not even asleep," but from the hesitating way in which I made the statement and from the laugh that went round, I felt that my words did not carry conviction to my hearers, so I went below to bury my disturbed feelings in the mysteries of the dining-room.

That dream knocked me out completely. We were nearly into port but I was almost afraid to get there, I would have liked a postponement of our landing for a day or two. Such feelings were foolish, however, and I shook them off as best I could, reasoning with myself that by no possibility could my friends have any idea that I was on board the " Servia." I slept but little that night and next noon we ran into port.

CHAPTER X.

New York!

We were back once more. Four puffing and fussy little tugs nosed the big steamer into her berth, and once more I stood on American soil. Would my dream be realized, where was the incomplete group waiting to receive me? I could not find it, and my heart felt glad, for, failing in one particular, my vision must necessarily be faulty as a whole. Securely stowed away in an inside pocket, I carried the diamond necklace for Annette, on which I did not propose to pay duty, and against the probability of having any trouble regarding it, I had fixed by the ring incident at Queenstown, I wore the ring myself, and intended as soon as I got on shore that I would have the stone re-set for ladies wearing. All the baggage which I had was one trunk and the bicycle, and these luckily got off the boat with the first lot of passengers' effects, and I ran them through the hands of the custom officers without much trouble.

In one hour's time from leaving the wharf I was at home, where, though late in the afternoon, I found not a single member of the family to supplement the surprise of the servants on seeing me thus suddenly turn up when they understood that I was on the other side of the Atlantic. I was scarcely in the house 15 minutes before my younger brother came in, and, what between myself and the pneumatic bicycle importation, I thought the boy would go pretty near crazy.

Dave was always a bright youngster, from the time he was a year old, and in 10 minutes' time, he had the machine at his fingers' ends, letting the air out of the valves, pumping it in again, screwing up this joint and loosening that one, and literally walking all over the wheel.

Suddenly he ceased his attention to the toy and came over to where I was rearranging my trunk, after taking out the things I had brought over for the family.

"Brother Will," he said, somewhat hesitatingly, "I want to tell you something."

"Well, go ahead, Dave," I said. "Isn't the machine all right?"

"Oh! it's a dandy, and I'm ever so much obliged to you for it, I deserve to be kicked for wasting the past half hour on it when I had something of importance maybe to tell you."

"Well, then make a break. What is it? You don't owe that confounded Wallis any more money, do you?" Dave sometimes got into small pecuniary difficulties, and I was invariably his confidant.

"A little, not much, but that's not what I meant, it's worse than that."

"Worse than that, well I had better not go away in such a hurry again. What's up now?"

"I don't think you had, leastwise you hadn't, I mean you were foolish—" here he stopped.

"——— the boy, I muttered, as I gave a vicious twist to some stuff in a corner of the trunk, "he's got the fool racket on, too."

Dave saw there was something wrong and he hesitated.

"Hand me a match and fire away with what you have got to say," I said.

He struck the match, and as I lighted a cigar blurted out:

"You know Annette Lascelles, don't you, brother Will?"

"Why, of course I do," I replied, in as suave a manner as possible, though mentally I was saying, "the young scallawag, he knows that as well as I do without asking."

"Well, you know that crazy-head lawyer feller, Somers, don't you, Will?"

"Yes, I know Dick Somers, but what the devil has he got to do with Miss Lascelles?"

"And you know Mr. Hicks, that stuffed so at mamma's reception, who looks like old Cleveland, only he hasn't any more manners than a boot-black?"

"What are you driving at, Dave? What has Hicks to do with Somers, or what have they both to do with Annette?" I dropped the name in-advertently, and at the same time dropped my cigar.

I stooped to pick it up, at the same time brushing the ashes off my coat sleeve.

Dave took advantage of my occupation and came right out with:

"They've got this much to do with her, one of them is going to marry Miss Lascelles, that's all. I thought you would like to know."

"I let the cigar lie and stared in blank astonishment at Dave, who was twirling one of the pedals of his machine round as if his life depended on making it go at the highest speed attainable.

"Dave," I said, "you're an ass."

"Maybe I am, but she's a bigger one if she marries one of those Jakes."

I scarcely knew whether to be angry at Dave's want of respect for Annette, or mollified at the disparagement of two of the men who, I must confess, I had had my eye on for some time past as being possible rivals for the favor of Annette."

"Come, come, Dave, you are mistaken," I said. "What makes you talk like that?"

"Well, brother Will, I didn't know but it would interest you, because I heard Cousin Bess say that it would, and she said you were a fool to go to Europe, and now that you're back, why don't you knock those chaps out? I like Annette, I do; she's a daisy, and she used to like you before you went away. Cousin Bess said that, too."

I was pretty nearly dumbfounded. I picked up my cigar, relighted it, got some writing materials, penned a note saying I was in New York and had brought her something from Europe, directed it to Annette, called Dave over and said:

"Dave, when you have delivered that letter and brought me an answer, you can bring me that bill from Wallis and any others you have. I'll look after them."

"You're not angry with me, Will, are you? Wallis' bill is only about $100."

"Certainly I'm not, you're a good boy for once, Dave. Now leg it, or ride it as fast as you can, and bring me an answer."

"I'll ride, and I'll get an answer or bust that pneumatic," he said, as, with the machine, he flung himself out of the room.

There was wonder without stint inside of the household an hour from that time. Questions without number were piled on me from every member of the family, but I kept my counsel and merely said that I got tired of the trip before it had commenced, and decided to return home.

## CHAPTER XI.

The answer.

Dave had brought it. I tore the little square envelope open with feverish impatience. There were three lines written across the small sheet of notepaper, and they were these: "Will Chaytor, you were not a fool to return to New York and Annette!"

"Dave, bring me that bill of yours, and any others your unlimited extravagance may have contracted," I said to my trusty messenger.

He was about to speak, but hesitated.

"Well, what's the matter, got a whole mountain of debt resting on your shoulders, Dave?"

"Brother Will, the bicycle is broke," he said, in a crestfallen way.

"Broken already! dead broke, is it, like yourself? Well, that's a pity; we must get it mended."

"I couldn't help it, Will; down at Desbrosses Street a big truck ran clear over the back wheel."

"Well, don't look so down in the mouth about it, Dave, I suppose you could not help it. The thing is easily mended."

"That's just what I told Miss Lascelles."

"The bicycle broke, then, when you were going; that was worse still."

"No, it didn't, either; the fool of an Irishman ran into me just as I got off the ferry."

"How in the name of sense, then, could you tell Miss Lascelles about it?"

"I didn't say I did. You told me not to be down in the mouth about it, and that's just what I told Miss Lascelles about you. I wasn't talkin' about the bicycle."

I grabbed him by the arm.

"What's that you say," I shouted; "you told Annette not to be down in the mouth about me? Dave, I'll kick you—"

"No, I didn't, either. I told Annette you were down in the mouth about her, or if you were not, you had lost an awful lot of money, or something. I told her you looked worried almost to death, but that I thought that she was so good and kind she could mend things up. That's almost what you told me about the bicycle."

I went over to a mirror and surveyed my physical appearance. I never appeared better in my life, never looked stronger or heartier.

"Dave, you're an ass—a double-distilled concentration of stupidity," I said.

"No, I aint, Will, I'll bet you I aint, for Annette said, 'Poor Will; he must have had a fearful bad trip'—I think she said fearful, and then she wrote that letter."

"Well, maybe you are not such a bad fellow, Dave, after all. Look those bills up, and I'll get them fixed, and get the bicycle fixed, too, and here, shake hands, Dave, my boy, you knock the special messenger service out anyhow."

Now, I suppose you fellows think you're going to get a taste of realistic

11

love-making. Not a bit of it; Annette was one of the most practical little bodies within the boundaries of New York. Two hours from the time I received her answer to my note I had knocked the chances of the other fellows—supposing they ever had any—into a good, old-fashioned cocked hat, and it was not the necklace, fine as it was, that did the business. I might have let the said necklace go, or a dozen of them for that matter, which fact on my discovering it forced me to acknowledge that, in sober earnest, I had very nearly made a big fool of myself, and to also acknowledge that I had found a wise little woman, as well as a loving one, in Annette.

At Nyack-on-the-Hudson, there is a typical American home where, on a ground-work of common sense, dwell love, honor, and happiness, and the greatest of these is happiness, because it is born of love and nurtured in honor.

" There's your story, boys, how does it suit you? I am sorry I could not tell it better than I have done. With Gil there, it's being a veracious tale will go a long way toward excusing its literary faults."

" I'm satisfied," said Gil, "but you forgot to tell us if, after chasing yourself across and back on the Atlantic, yourself, or rather Annette and the chaser, got married."

" Gil would like the whole courtship, marriage-service, and honeymoon served up with extra salad dressing. Come, Gil, you're not so dumb as all that; can't you understand they got married, did Will and Annette, and lived happily ever after at Nyack," said Laurie.

" Don't we pass that place going down the river?" queried Gilbert.

" Yes, very shortly."

" Well, then, suppose Mac shows us the exact spot where the heroine of this romance of real life lives," put in Gil.

" Oh! you can't see the house from the river," the writer remarked.

" I thought not, that's generally the way with interesting things of this sort," and as Gil spoke he got up and went over to the rail.

" Mac, is that tale as true as Chester's ? Give it straight, old man," asked Laurie.

" As far as I know of Chester's story, the one I have told is truer. I never saw his summer girl flame."

" Nor I. I suppose he had no compunctions about taking us into his confidence, as it is several years since his trip to Lake George," said Laurie, and then he also went over to the rail, as he remarked, to "take a snap-shot of Nyack" when we should reach that place.

# CHAPTER XI.

## HOME AGAIN.

It was but a short half-hour from the finishing of the last of the quartette of stories, when the high banks at West Point rose up to the right. As the steamer passed this historic spot a cheer from a group of cadets belonging to the famous military college at that place greeted the wash from her paddle wheels on the rocks of the Point. The Indian fighters of the future to the number of about twenty were enjoying a swim, some of them being in the water and others spread over the rocks. In a few moments they were away behind. To one-half of the " Quartette " this noted river trip was entirely new, and the cameras had to do heavy duty in catching the numerous objects of interest along the time-honored shore, the flotillas of canal barges, and the various pleasure craft dotting the broad bosom of the river, Poughkeepsie, Newburgh, Storm King Mountain, standing out bluff and hearty against the gray-blue sky; the old-time abiding places of Washington Irving and the many other notable characters in literature and history, whose names are indissolubly linked with this beautiful stream. Then the " Palisades " rose up dun colored and impressive in the distance, and not the less interesting as we passed them. Up-stream came the noted old river-boat, the " Mary Powell," and then as the great " Babylon " of the New World, represented by the cities of New York, Jersey City, and Brooklyn, was approached, lying under a hazy mist which rolled in from the ocean, the shipping of all kinds increased in number, and as the broadside of Gotham crept toward us, or rather as we swept down upon it, the head and front of marine interest came into view in the shape of the " White Squadron," which we had last seen at Boston on the commencement of our journeyings. " Uncle Sam's " great cruisers were lying at anchor in mid-stream, and as we ran by them, all eyes were bent on the stately vessels lying at ease on the calm waters of the royal stream, their square yards, black smoke-stacks, and white hulls forming a splendid spectacle, interesting alike to the eye of the unsophisticated landsman and the professional seaman. Inside of a few minutes from reaching it, our boat ran into her berth, and once more we were on solid earth in the city of New York. Only for a few minutes, however, for it was nearly six o'clock, and, making straight for the Pennsylvania Railroad ferries, we were soon on the Jersey shore and sampling the rough-and-tumble pavements of Jersey City. As long as daylight lasted the programme was to go ahead. So, through Jersey City, and across the low-lying lands between that great centre and Newark, the trio of riders made their way. The road connecting the two large cities may be a fairly good one in point of surface, but we found it a most abominably foul one in the way of olfactory embellishment. Of all the evil smells met with during the course of the three weeks' trip, those of the seven or eight miles' stretch between Jersey City and Newark were most decidedly the worst.

Once is enough to travel that dismal stretch of country. By the side of the road stretch long vistas of marsh-land covered with waving masses of flags and rushes, suggesting scenes and incidents such as in our younger days we had delighted in dwelling upon in blood-curdling creations of the realistic novelist and crime concocter. The proximity of numerous hog-slaughtering and like establishments was most offensively demonstrated through more than one of our very acute senses, and it was with feelings of relief that we saw the heavenward climbing chimney of the Clarke thread mills gradually grow taller and taller as we approached the busy centre of industry known as Newark.

At Newark supper was in order and Heaven deliver us from ever having to sup or dine or sample any kind of meal in that burgh again. The sample we had of supper, decided us to push on to Elizabeth, some four miles nearer Philadelphia, for a stopping-place for the night, and into this latter town we rolled about 10 P. M., and half an hour later went to sleep to the music of endless moving trains on the Central Railroad of New Jersey.

Next morning the " Quartette " was most inexcusably lazy. It was nine o'clock before breakfast was finished and the magnificent road leading to Westfield and Plainfield tackled. Being Saturday, it was imperative that the State of New Jersey, lying between us and our much-desired homes in Philadelphia, should be crossed. It was an 80-mile ride, but, on the last day of the trip, and hardened as we were by three weeks of work on the road, this did not appear as anything too much to cover, and under clear skies and over one of the finest roads in America, running through West-field to Plainfield, the "Quartette" made the best time of the whole trip.

Being the route followed by the great century runs between Newark and Philadelphia, the ride across New Jersey needs but slight description. Reaching Plainfield and Bound Brook too early for dinner, the enjoying of the mid-day meal was postponed until Hopewell was reached, and at this quiet little hamlet the weary inner man was refreshed after a manner that is well and favorably known to cyclers who make the journey a-wheel between the two great metropolitan centres of New York and Philadelphia. Dinner over, a half-hour's rest followed, and then "on for Trenton" was the word, and on for Trenton we went, over roads that, built of red clay, were passable enough, but not nearly so satisfactory riding as the grand highways leading out of Elizabeth and ending at Plainfield.

Historic Trenton! We reached it, we went through it, we did not stop in it, it was old ground to us, but straight down that well-known composition-block paved street to the long bridge across the Delaware went the "Quartette," and as the evening shadows commenced to assert themselves in the eastern sky, the Pennsylvania shore was gained, and into Bristol, after an abominably rutty and sandy ride, with one mistake made as to the road, the now slightly weary pedalers pushed their way.

Some refreshment was in order at Glosson's noted hostelry, and then down the Bristol Pike with the appetite of expectation whetted, the "Quartette " rode and walked toward the "City of Homes." The sun had set. Darkness was falling faster than we bargained for, and faster than the miserably surfaced road rendered agreeable. Side-path riding was all that could be done, and side-path walking was as often as not the order of march. The swiftly-rushing trains on the Pennsylvania Railroad between Philadelphia and New York passed us in either direction, their on-rushing making mock of our comparatively slow advance. Then night fell, and as we drew near the environs of Frankford and its aggregation of cobblestones and vile street railway tracks, the practical soul of Gil Wiese rebelled against work fit only for "hewers of wood and drawers of water," and he proposed that for the balance of the ride into the "overgrown village" the steel highway should be laid under requisition. The writer seconded the motion, and down to one of the way stations, through what was pitch darkness, floundered the "Quartette." A resident of the locality informed us that the next train did not stop.

"Flag it," said Gil Wiese.

"You can do so by a green light," said the local citizen.

Forthwith Gil raised a green lantern secured from the station, and mounting a truck on the platform, he swung the signal frantically round his head as the great eye of the locomotive came down the track.

We were aboard the train in a jiffy, machines and all, and, curiously enough, found the baggage-master a cycler and a rider of a "Hickory" wheel. He made things comfortable for us for the 10 minutes' trip across the city to the much-frequented "Zoo" station, where, piling out, five minutes later saw the "Quartette" safe within the precincts of the Pennsylvania Bicycle Club.

Kind and long-suffering reader, we have finished; our trip is at an end, our bicycles lie in their old accustomed racks in the wheel-room of the club-house; they are, as we are ourselves, soiled and travel-stained, the blue and gold on their handle-bars is faded, and in one instance missing, lost amid the New Hampshire hills, but they are, as we are ourselves, safe at home.

"The sweetest, dearest spot of all the rest,"

and over them hangs the club banner, and in blue emblems, on a field of gold, we read the club song.

I.

"Tender and true
The gold and the blue
Waves over ' Pennsylvania,'
And rolling high
The grand old cry
Rings out ' Pennsylvania.'

II.

"With hand and with heart,
Though spread far apart,
Still it is ' Pennsylvania;'
Still ' tender and true,'
The gold and the blue,
Still we are ' Pennsylvania.'

III.

"The blue and the gold
Can never grow old
For us or for ' Pensylvania;'
For tender and true,
'Neath the gold and the blue,
' We're nothing if not ' Pennsylvania.'"

[THE END.]

www.ingramcontent.com/pod-product-compliance
Lightning Source LLC
Chambersburg PA
CBHW031447270326
41930CB00007B/908